Our Journey Together

Seventy-one years of marriage:
stories of life and love

Blessings to Jim charles

Ruth Garber Rohrer

July 2015

Elmer Herr Rohrer

Ruth Herr Garber Rohrer

Cover photo near Gunnison, Colorado

Dedication

We thankfully dedicate this book to our family as a gift of memories and love. They each contributed to our "Journey."

Photographs are mostly from family collections.

Quotes from Scripture are from THE HOLY BIBLE, NEW INTERNATIONAL VERSION® NIV®
Copyright © 1973, 1978, 1984 by International Bible Society®
Used by permission. All rights reserved worldwide.

ISBN: 978-0-9892992-3-7

Printed: May 2015
Printed by: Executive Printing Co., Inc: Elm, Pa.

Contents

Part Three—Our Journey Together

Ruth's Introduction

My Japanese friend, Chie Layman, recently assured me that people want to know how Mennonite children grew up so long ago; what happened in our homes and especially on the farms; what influenced us to know God and to make good decisions.

"Every person should write about their early memories, and it should be done while they are young enough to remember their feelings," Chie advised.

"Our Journey Together" is an attempt to share these facts as we review our story from 1920 to 2015 in this joint collection of "word pictures."

In February 2001, Goshen College Extension Services offered a short course on "Writing My Life's Story" in Sarasota, Florida. This appealed to me because I had already been thinking about doing that during the time we were in Florida that winter. So God blessed me with the encouragement to start this exciting assignment. Dolores Wilson was the professor and the class of eight students made good use of the six sessions on story writing. I am very grateful for the guidance and suggestions she gave to us. She helped us realize that whereas artists paint pictures with paints, writers paint pictures with words. The more one writes, the more one realizes there is to write about.

Elmer's Introduction

Dear Daddy,

This blank book is a gift to you but it is for the purpose of you giving a gift of yourself to your children and grandchildren.

Over the years you have had many experiences growing up as a child, learning to work, developing values and faith in God, learning from your own mistakes and from the mistakes of others. You've lived through the teen years and the young adult years, you dated, you married, you began a family, developed a farm, became owner of the farm, then sold one and bought another and later sold it and gradually you moved into retirement, you've had decision after decision to make. You and Mother had 7 children to train up in the fear of the Lord.

There have been thoughts and dreams, some expressed and some, no doubt, just kept to yourself.

I know that writing is not an everyday activity for you but perhaps the Lord will give you the grace and inspiration to sit down and begin putting in this book some of your life experiences, memories and thoughts that would be deeply cherished and appreciated by those of us who are your offspring.

No need to be concerned about the order in which you write things. Just write an approximate date or time period in which it occured.

Thank you, Daddy, for this gift of love. May it not feel like a burden to you. Anything you share will be counted as a tremendous gift!

With love and deep appreciation,
Linda
Nov 1999

Linda dear,

You gave me a blank book 15 years ago and I have read your tender plea a number of times, only to lay the book down again. I thought to myself, "I am not a writer, but I am "somebody." It's been said that God doesn't make "junk." So this time when I read your note, it seemed to come to me with new intensity; if I am going to do this, the time is now. You basically gave me an outline to get me started. Thank you!

Love, Daddy

Part One

Elmer Writes

My Grandpa and Grandma Herr, Rudolph and Susan.

My grandparents, Clinton and Fianna Rohrer

Here I am at age one year, 1921

My parents' wedding picture - Elmer Barto Rohrer and Rebecca Herr

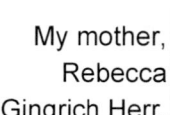

My mother, Rebecca Gingrich Herr.

CHAPTER ONE

My Family-
This I Have Been Told

On March 5, 1920, in the midst of a snow blizzard, Dr. B. F. Good received word that a baby was to be born at the home of Elmer B. and Rebecca G. Rohrer. The doctor decided to trust the horse rather than the Buick for the three-mile trek to their home.

Later that day Elmer Herr Rohrer was added to the number of 8th generation of Rohrers who descended from Jacob and Anna Rohrer who emigrated to America in 1734. This gave me a Swiss-German background. Following Jacob Rohrer there were four generations of John Rohrers. These were followed by my grandfather, Clinton Heistand Rohrer, born January 4, 1860, and my father, Elmer Barto Rohrer who was born on March 4, 1887. On October 6, 1910, he married my mother, Rebecca Gingrich Herr, born January 12, 1888.

I also became a member of the 9th generation of Herrs, dating back to the immigrant, Rev. Hans Herr. So on that wintry day of March 5, 1920, I was lovingly greeted by my parents and two wide eyed sisters. The oldest, Kathryn, was born December 20, 1911, and Ruth was born on January 28, 1917. My parents had lived on Manor Avenue in Millersville, Pennsylvania for five years prior to moving to the farm on Wabank Road where I was born.

About 1915 my parents signed a deed to a 25 acre parcel of open Herr land. On this land they built a red brick house, barn and small chicken house and hog pen at a total cost of $7,000. This property was about a half mile south of the east end of Millersville. The Wabank Road was on the south and west border of this farm. This land is presently occupied by the Oak Leaf Manor Retirement Community. In 1970 the farm buildings were demolished and a bank building replaced them.

My ancestors were largely members of the Mennonite and Brethren faith groups. My parents and grandparents were of Mennonite persuasion. In May 1734, Jacob and Anna Rohrer were deeded a land grant signed by Thomas Penn, of 293 acres of land located west of Manheim, Pennsylvania and east of Mount Joy, between the village of Sporting Hill and the present-day Erisman Mennonite Church. This land stayed in the Rohrer family for several generations.

(Note: More history of "The Rohrer Family of Rapho, 1734-2000" may be found at the Lancaster Mennonite Information Center).

Early Memories

The first memory that comes to my mind is walking to Sunday school at Millersville Mennonite Church with my two sisters. That was the church I was carried into as a baby and we still worship there today. At that early time period church services alternated, one week at Millersville and the next week at Rohrerstown. But Sunday school met every Sunday afternoon. After October 1924, services were held weekly at both churches.

At that time there was a mixed scene in the church parking lot. Both automobiles and a few horse-drawn carriages parked in the horse sheds. My parents made the change from horse to car when they bought a new 1917 Overland 90 touring car. This car served the family until 1928, when they purchased a one year old demonstrator Willys Knight four-door sedan. As we drove to church that first Sunday I sensed something about Dad's demeanor that was different. He did not park at his usual spot. Not wanting to make a display, he found a more remote spot. The old car, the Overland, then served as a "truck" to take produce to be sold in the Lancaster markets. Now and then a calf was pushed into the back seat area and taken to the Lancaster stockyards to be sold.

There were times, I remember, as growing boys we would sit behind that wheel and pretend we were going places. The time came when I was allowed to take the Overland to the fields. So that was where I learned to drive the 1917 Overland touring car. But it was in the 1927 Willys Knight at a later date that I took my driver's test. Then I could drive on the road. What a pleasure.

The Overland car had a feature that wasn't talked about. It had a cutout – one could press a pedal on the floorboard to open the cutout and bypass the muffler. It created a straight exhaust, and it was loud! I don't know why that feature was created in the first place – maybe the designers also liked loud engine noises! Anyway, this feature became illegal to use, so it was unhooked. But I have a special memory about that feature. It was cherry picking time at Great Aunt Lizzie's sweet cherry trees, over along Columbia Avenue, at Herr's Ice Plant. With just a little coaxing, Dad found a way to keep that cutout open by placing a stone under the lid. According to the grin on Dad's face, I think he enjoyed the noise too, as we drove to and from Aunt Lizzie's place.

Dad, Mother and Kathryn with their horse and carriage.

Before I was born my parents used a horse and carriage. Next came the 1917 Overland Touring car similar to the car pictured on the right, and then the 1927 Willys Knight, similar to the car pictured below.

The home farm on Wabank Road, outside Millersville. My birthplace.

Pulling tobacco plants.

Paul and I get an early start, "milking" our calves.

CHAPTER TWO

Growing Up On The Farm

My memory gives me a visual picture of Grandpa and Grandma Herr driving in the lane in a buggy being pulled by their faithful horse, Cap. That other boy is my younger brother, Paul, born on June 10, 1922. After unhitching Cap and putting him in the horse stable we are ready to plant corn. This was done by hand and Dad was already in that six-acre field just below the garden. The corn was checker planted. Dad was marking off the rows so Grandpa would know where to drop the seeds.

I think I hear you asking, "What do you mean by marking off the rows?" This was done with a tool we called a scorer. A scorer can best be described as a wooden frame with two posts pointing down, spaced thirty-six inches apart; on each post a nine inch U-shaped blade was bolted. Two horses pulled it; the person driving the horse and guiding the scorer held on to two arms or handles that extended out the back of the implement. Marking or scoring the rows meant one trip through the field for each row both long-ways and cross-ways. This method of spacing the hills thirty-six inches apart both ways meant the corn could then be cultivated both ways. After the field was scored it was ready to plant.

The plan was simple; drop three grains, kick some ground, enough to cover the grain and move on; drop three more grains, give a kick and move on. This meant all able-bodied persons that could help, would help. I think my mother helped plant corn, but Grandma Herr stayed in the house, probably to make dinner. It's planting time and I hope you get the picture.

Now it is time for Grandpa and Grandma to return to their home in Millersville, the house where my parents lived before they moved to the farm. Grandpa brings Cap from the horse stable. I am now big enough to hold the buggy shafts up while Grandpa backs Cap into them, and off they go. It's been a good day.

My mind seems to be flooded with more memories about or with Grandpa and Grandma Herr. On occasion we would drop in to visit them unannounced and there was Grandpa seated by the table, with that red checkered tablecloth that seemed to be quivering, reading his Bible. Christmas dinners at Grandma's were enjoyed by all; aunts, uncles and cousins. A typical scene after a good Christmas dinner was the aunts and the big girl cousins taking care of the leftover food, brushing the crumbs off the tablecloth and washing the dishes. The boy cousins rushed out to see Uncle Roy's new Reo car. The uncles and Grandpa gathered in the living room just to talk and share some stories.

We boys came back in the house just in time to hear Uncle Roy start a story. Now when he told a story you could almost see it happen. "Let me take you back to pioneer days," he said. "They were clearing the land. The trees were cut and some stumps remained. It was spring time; time to plow the land. The horses were well rested and frisky and raring to go. All went well until the plow hit a stump, right dab, smack in the middle. It sprung open, pulling the plow and the driver through--well almost. That stump sprung back together again and caught the driver by the seat of his pants. They never would have gotten that stump out without those rawhide suspenders." Well, that story won the liar's contest that year.

Now the date is December 25, 1930, and the families have gathered at Grandpa's as usual, except for Mother and Dad. Earlier that morning Mother sensed a need to go to the hospital, so off they went. Sometime later that afternoon Dad seemed pleased to say he now has another son. The news was a complete surprise to both Paul and me. So Robert completed this Rohrer family.

Another thought about Christmas was the myth of Santa Claus which we were told about. We made our yearly trip to the department stores but we were not encouraged to sit on Santa's lap. I do remember getting a wind-up train set one year. That was probably for both Paul and me.

It was while Grandma and Grandpa Herr were on a rail trip to Denver, Colorado and points west with the Oliver Shenk Tour Group, that Paul and I accepted the responsibility to feed their small flock of chickens and make sure that Cap was also fed. This meant a half-mile hike to Millersville each day. I well remember the pocket knives from Denver, Colorado, that we were gifted. The time came when Grandpa also made the move to have Cap replaced with a new 1928 Model A Ford Coupe. Imagine the excitement we boys must have shown when we told our sisters we were going 40 miles an hour in Grandpa's new car.

One day Dad was plowing with a pair of horses and one of the horses fell into a sink hole, unable to get out. Our neighbor, George Herr, working in a nearby field, saw the problem and took the opportunity to offer a hand. I don't remember how they challenged the task, but I remember the other horse showed tears when he saw his partner in that hole; and a whinny of cheer when the horse was freed. Even the animals have a sense of empathy.

We were now in the midst of what became known as the Great Depression of the nineteen thirties. Many banks were closed and the stock market crashed. This resulted in many people being out of work and few jobs available. My parents' savings were not lost; only some interest was lost for a period of time. But we did live frugally. The tobacco prices were greatly depressed. Dad had a plan. He would not sell the crop, but pack the tobacco in cases, just like the tobacco companies did, and wait `til the prices rebound. This was repeated the next year. He, in fact, bought and "packed" a neighbor's crop also.

Mother and Dad were not in agreement in this venture. Mother could get vocal when she was upset and I heard some of this at times. I may have said, or thought in my mind, "If marriage has to be like this, I will not marry." I am happy to say that their relationship healed over time. After a few years that tobacco did sell at a very satisfactory price. But how do you put a price on relationship?

During the depression people were too proud to beg and were willing to work as harvest hands on the farm for one dollar per day. My parents experienced frozen bank accounts for a period of time. But we farm families had the advantage of raising much of our food. Hams were smoked and hung in the attic. Food from the garden was canned for winter use.

The family car registered only two thousand miles per year. In spite of the hardships, it was still important to exchange visits with aunts and uncles. The parting words were, "Now I want you folks to come to our house next." Or depending on the area they lived in they may have said, "Youen's come back soon." Those family visits were enjoyed by all.

But there was a difference, I sensed, between the Herr and the Rohrer grandparents. Grandpa and Grandma Herr were so jovial and kind, while Grandma Rohrer was so frail and somber. Grandpa Rohrer was tall and well built with a cud of tobacco in his mouth and a big lump on his neck. His greeting to me was, "Hi, bouva," with a chuckle. This was Pennsylvania Dutch for "Hi, boy." (We never used Pennsylvania Dutch in our home except when the butcher came. Then Dad would carry on a conversation with him in Dutch. Mother understood Dutch, but didn't speak it.)

But there is more to be said, something that was not family talk in those early years. When I was a teenager, a cousin who lived next door to Grandpa's shared with me that there was a problem. Grandpa had an alcohol problem and at times he became very abusive. I never saw any evidence of his abusiveness, but I suspect that explains Grandma's demeanor. Grandpa Rohrer struggled with that problem until the latter years of his life. He did find victory over the problem by surrendering his wallet to his daughter with whom he lived at the time. He found grace and peace with Christ, his Lord and Savior. At Grandpa's funeral at age 95, there was a note of joy for a victory won.

Another memory comes to mind. This time Uncle Earl and Uncle Oliver Rohrer and Grandpa Rohrer came in the drive in Uncle Earl's big black Hudson, the kind that had a couple extra seats that folded and fit against the back of the front seat. It had high wheels and skinny tires. Dad joined them to take Grandpa to the Will's Eye Hospital in Philadelphia. A cataract operation in those days was not a simple operation. We were told Grandpa had to lie on his back, with sand bags on either side of his head, with the command "Do not move" for an extended period of time. Yes, his vision was improved but it was tunnel vision and he became blind in his later years.

There's more to tell regarding my boyhood days on the farm. The "checker" method of planting corn by hand was soon replaced when a horse-drawn, John Deere 999, two-row checker planter was purchased. A horse-drawn manure spreader replaced the plank wagon and the hand and fork method of spreading it. The farm was divided into four nearly equal sized fields, and we followed a four year rotation of corn, tobacco, wheat and hay. The livestock consisted of a stable full of 8 or 9 cows, one stock bull, a few pigs, two horses and a small flock of chickens. We children were expected to help as soon as we were old enough.

Let me share a little ditty that I can almost hear now as Dad walked to the barn in the early morning hours: "Oh, it's hard to be a farmer and I should surely know, for I planted a whole handful of feathers and not one of them did grow, did grow." Oh, yes, he did enjoy the farm and the family. Sometimes he would join us in a ball game. It was fun to see Dad run. The ball games happened only after the work was done. I also remember practicing catching the ball by throwing the ball against the gable end of the barn and running to catch the rebound. I think of the time when Paul became the water boy and I was helping to load the hay. I was growing up.

My first attempt with the land roller; a typical first job for a boy in the field. Paul watches and looks forward to his turn.

We put the ladder on a hay wagon so we could reach the top of the barn. That's me on the higher ladder. A salesman stopped by and said it looks like I have more paint on my clothes than on the barn. Paul stayed closer to the ground.

Mother and the chicks.

There was pride in loading a nice square load of loose hay.

We used a threshing machine with a self feeder
similar to this one.

CHAPTER THREE

Harvest Time and Summer Fun

Hay-making and wheat harvest time hold special memories for me. We cut the grass with a 6 foot horse-drawn mower. When it was partially dry we used a hay tedder to aerate the grass. When sufficiently dry, we switched to the dump rake to gather the hay and dump it in horizontal rows across the field. Next step was heaping the hay into piles. This was done with a short-handled four-pronged fork. Next was loading the hay on the wagon, with one man walking on either side of the wagon using long handled pitch forks. Two men were on the wagon. There was pride in being able to load a nice square load of loose hay.

Next came early July and wheat harvest. Uncle Rudy Herr, Mother's brother, came from the south side of Millersville with his four-mule team and the binder to cut the wheat. Another four-mule team came with a wagon plus 2 or 3 day laborers to help gather the sheaves into the barn. As a water boy I had to be on the alert or most any one of those men would target my bare feet as a spittoon for their tobacco juice. As I got older we also helped Uncle Rudy on his farm.

A few weeks later the threshing rig came to our farm. I heard the whistle and there he comes around the bend. Yes, that is Harry Frey with his Avery steam engine pulling a threshing machine, with a straw baler in tow. First he pushed the baler into the barn, then the threshing machine. Now it's time to line up that steam engine square with the separator. A long endless belt is placed over a pulley on the separator and the other end on the flywheel of the steam engine. They inch the steam engine back just enough to make the belt taut. By now the other men who travel with the crew have all the bearings greased. Two short toots from the steam whistle and the action begins. The wheat sheaves have been stored in the barn, waiting for this day. Several men relay the sheaves to the man feeding the separator; another man bags the grain; two men are tending the baler and another couple of people are taking the straw bales away and stacking them neatly in the mow. The water boy makes his rounds; sometimes it is lemonade. So on and on it went until that steam whistle gave the dinner call.

Now we are changing scenes. A dozen or more men are gathered around the pump trough, waiting their turn to wash up. There seems to be plenty of conversation and laughter. Soon they are gathered around the table. A prayer is offered and the food is served. The housewives know these men are hungry, so there is plenty of food, including pies. They also know that this threshing gang goes to the neighboring farms and there seems to be a rating system among them, based on the dinners served. I am sure my mother's rated near the top.

It's now August and it's time to harvest the tobacco crop. The tobacco is cut and allowed a couple hours to wilt. Then five or six stalks are speared unto a lathe and laid aside to be loaded on a ladder wagon and taken to the tobacco shed where it is hung on rails to dry. The heat near the roof seemed to open one's sweat glands from head to toe. The tobacco hung there until the winter months.

Soon it is silo filling time. I remember it as a time I would look forward to eagerly. The "neighbor help neighbor" system of labor exchange built a good working relationship among the neighbors, and it was a pleasure. The corn was cut by hand, using a corn chopper: cut a small armful, lay it on the ground and repeat. There were several men cutting. Soon a two-horse team pulling a flat bed wagon and one or two men loaded the corn stalks on the wagon and headed off to the silo to unload one armful after another into the ensilage cutter, which then blew it up a pipe into the silo. It was important to have a man in the silo to move the distributor pipe around and level the silage. We all knew that when that call for dinner came the food would be good and plentiful.

Shredding fodder on the home farm with a
9-horse-power Domestic engine.

Corn that was not needed to fill the silo was cut by hand and placed into shocks to be husked at a later date. I later learned that Ruth's mother used a word picture to describe corn shocks. She called them "Corn ladies, with their skirts spread wide and their faces on the other side."

Corn shocks remind me of hunting season. Dad enjoyed hunting rabbits and it seemed to please him that we boys could join him. Three people could cover a much wider path than one. I was gifted a Daisy BB gun and cautioned never to point that gun at any person. Ring-necked pheasants were legal game and they presented a challenge. Later I was gifted a single barrel shot gun. Soon I learned I needed to take a more careful aim. Oh, no, I just missed another one!

A year or two later I was old enough to have a hunting license. Here is the plan. I could now join Dad and Uncle Rudy on the opening day to hunt at Mother's cousin Dan Herr's farm. The ground cover and the game were in abundance. Let me say this as modestly as I can. I shot 4 rabbits, 2 cock birds and one squirrel and only used 7 shells that day. I have one more hunting story. Those corn shocks are now large fodder shocks in the field; the corn has been husked and put in cribs to dry. Those fodder shocks offered good protection for rabbits. That is until my dog, we called him Penny, circled the shock and if he then entered the shock, we needed to be ready. Yes, there he went. Paul got that rabbit.

❧

It was now winter time. I was now big enough to help my sisters milk the cows. The horses were fed and curried and it's breakfast time. After a good breakfast of a couple dippy eggs and toast, or perhaps fried mush and pork "puddins" we were off to school. But on a Saturday, after a few clean up chores at the barn, I would join Dad in the nice warm tobacco stripping room. Some days prior to this, on a humid day, the tobacco laths were taken from the shed and hung in the dampening cellar. From there they went to the stripping room. Here the stalks were pulled from the laths and the leaves were stripped from the stem, graded for size and quality and tied into hands and pressed into bales. It was now ready to sell.

There was a tree near the stripping room where the sparrows and starlings gathered. This gave an opportunity to use that BB gun. I would open the door a crack, enough to stick the barrel out, take aim and shoot. Sometimes I shot under the bird, and missed again. That changed when we advanced to the 22-single-shot rifle, because that bullet travels a straighter trajectory than the BB does. We could take a more accurate aim and hit the mark. Even Dad would take a turn sometimes.

Along with winter came those sledding and skating gatherings. The road past our house was the favorite hill. The

Herrs, the Eshbachs, the Keagys and the Rohrers gathered there. Sometimes there was a good crust on the snow and we would sled in the fields. I am not sure that we ever settled the debate between the Lightening Glider and the Flexible Flyer sleds. But I sure did like my little Flexible Flyer.

Skating! That too was fun, sometimes at Hostetter's pond or at my Great Uncle Christ Herr's ice plant ponds. That's where the young guys took their lady friends to skate.

Summer activities followed winter fun. There was free time between seed time and harvest and we wanted to swim. Going to Maple Grove public swimming pool was not an option. That cost money. The farm on the west side of ours had a stream flowing through the meadow. Several of us boys made an assumption that Bill would not care. So we built a dam and we had our own swimming hole. This continued for some time until one day Bill showed up and said, in not too kindly a voice, "Have fun, but tomorrow the dam comes down." And it did. You see Bill and his wife did not have any children. They didn't understand.

On the south side of our farm was the Eshbach farm and they too had a stream. So we built another dam, this time with their help. That's where I learned to swim. Sometime later the neighbors up stream built a good sized pond for fire protection. At the pond we could also dive into the water. I felt accomplished when I completed eight laps around that pond.

In my early years it was not unusual for a hobo, or he might be called a tramp or a bum, to stop by and want a meal. Or he might ask to sleep in the barn that night. The practice at our home was that we allowed him to sleep here, but he needed to place his matches on a log on the porch. In the winter time they would sleep in an empty horse stall on a bed of straw. Other times, they were upstairs in the barn. Sometimes they were invited into the house for breakfast, other times they ate on the porch. We even had names for a few of them. There was "Straitie," "Red Finegan," and "Henner Young." Henner Young would split some wood at times as a thank you. There were days that Dad would hire Red to help in the tobacco harvest. One time there was a hobo that carried a couple of stringed instruments in his bag. We were entertained that evening as we gathered in the tobacco stripping room. Even the girls joined us that time. We also had peddlers who walked the roads, going from house to house selling red handkerchiefs, thread, shoe strings, tea towels and other small items.

Dad with me in our kitchen in later years.

My siblings with their spouses. L-R: Lorraine and Bob Rohrer, Edith
and Paul Rohrer, Ruth and Elmer Rohrer, Kathryn and Mylin Herr,
Ruth and John Siegrist.

My parents built this house on Wabank Road, south of Millersville, Pa and moved there in 1915, before I was born. In 1955 they built a smaller home just up the road, and Bob and Lorraine lived in this house for a while. Mylin and Kathryn lived here for a while, too. The property was torn down and replaced with a bank building in the 1980s.

CHAPTER FOUR

The House We Called Home

Let me tell you something about the house we called home. I see a cook stove in the corner, enclosed by four folding doors, which were closed in summertime to keep some of the heat out of the kitchen. We didn't have a summer kitchen, but the doors around the stove helped control the heat in the house. The time is mid October, and the oven is stuffed full of ears of field corn left to dry until it has just the right aroma. Then we will gather around the kitchen and shell the corn by hand. I remember going along with Dad to the Stoneroad Mill (the miller's name was Mr. Stoneroad) to have that corn ground by the old millstone method. The end product was a good supply of corn meal. We used the corn meal for evening meals of mush and milk, followed by a breakfast of fried mush and molasses. Even now, on a cold evening, I enjoy a good serving of corn pone with syrup and milk.

Back to the kitchen – beside the cook stove was a woodbox, which we boys needed to fill, but also a good place to curl up on a cold evening. There is a slate counter top surrounding the sink, an oval-shaped dinner table with Dad at the head end and two boys on the bench back of the table. My two sisters are around the other end with Bobby on the highchair between Mother and Dad.

I see the dining room table extended. This time it's not the threshing gang, nor the silo fillers, but it is aunts, uncles and cousins around this long table. It is after dinner on Sunday. The boys soon go to explore the outdoors. The men and later the ladies find the comfort of the living room and the girls go across the front hall to the parlor.

Now there is something different about the rooms at the front of the house. The trim around the windows and doors is chestnut wood, "a touch of class." Another thing to notice is a 4-foot square metal grate in the floor. On a cold winter day heat would come from the coal-fired furnace in the basement, and there was also a smaller register in the ceiling to let a little heat upstairs.

That parlor was used much more when Kathryn began dating and in due time it was followed by my sister, Ruth as well. Over those times the sounds that wafted up the stair steps varied; one time a jew's harp, maybe a mouth organ, plus some stringed instruments, as well as the piano with voices singing hymns. Kathryn was dating Mylin Herr for some time now. He could play a number of instruments. "Perhaps that will be a match," I thought. The same could have been said about Bill Conrad and his friend Helen. They had been friends and often enjoyed dates together with Kathryn and Mylin and visited in our home. Kathryn and Mylin got married on October 26, 1935, when I was fifteen years old.

I remember a bit of conversation about family life after Kathryn was married. One of us young teen-aged boys made the comment that we would certainly miss her, but now the pieces of pie will be bigger.

By this time the aroma in the living room had changed. Some of my uncles seemed to enjoy puffing away on their favorite brand of cigar. It was enjoyed by some and endured by others. Dad did chew tobacco early in my lifetime. I think it was called "Mr. Goodbite."

Another observation you could have made on this tour was you did not see any coal oil lamps or electric light bulbs in the house. But we did have lights in each room in the house as well in each stable at the barn and in the chicken house. We had an acetylene gas lighting system. The gas was produced in what we called an acetylene gas plant, a blend of union carbide and water. This produced a gas that was piped to each lamp. To turn on the lights, we opened the gas valve, then flipped a little lever that created a spark to light the system. That system was replaced with electricity early in the 1940's.

We need to say a few words about that wall telephone. It was a party line phone system. You notice that crank on the side of the box. It was used to call the operator with one long ring, or any of the four or five families on your party line. Each party knew their code. We answered to 2 long and 2 short rings. The telephone was not a good place to  share any private information. Your neighbor may have been listening in on their phone at the same time.

Now as we re-enter the kitchen, I get a flashback of myself standing by that wash bowl. I hear Mother saying, "Stand up straight, Elmer. Square your shoulders." She didn't want her son to grow up with a humped back.

As we go upstairs, the room on the left was my parent's bedroom, plus the crib in which all five of us took our turn. Across the hall was the girls' room. They benefitted from one half of that small heat register on the floor. The other half was in the hallway. Then back the short hall was the boys' room above the kitchen. The stovepipe that came up in that room supplied a little heat. Opposite the front stairway was the bathroom. Notice those four claw feet on that bathtub. At the end of the hall was a clothes closet with some shelving for books. On these shelves Dad had some books giving guidance for the operation and care of the internal combustion engine. These were rather new at this time. That fourth bedroom was the guest room. Had I pulled the covers back on my bed to show you the mattress, no, it was not a Serta, but one that was filled with straw. I do remember helping Mother empty it into a horse stall for bedding and then refilling it with fresh straw.

Had I taken you to the attic, you would have noticed the smell of patent smoked ham hanging there to cure. That tasted so good! We conclude this tour with a trip to the basement. You notice the Fairbank Morris hit and miss gas engine that was used to pump water and also run the washing machine that was down there. In the back cellar you see the furnace and the coal bin with a chute from the outside where the truck unloaded an order of coal for the furnace. Another doorway opened into the arch cellar, where the potatoes and apples were kept in the wintertime.

Tuesday was market day. Mother enjoyed her day on market. She enjoyed meeting the customers and the fellow stand holders. She also made a contribution to the family needs by selling some produce, eggs and a few dressed chickens weekly. The garden produce was sold seasonally. Paul and I got some sales experience going from door to door in Millersville selling asparagus in the spring and it was repeated by selling celery in the fall.

Another glimpse at the market house scene in the springtime would show Mother almost hidden by a big tub of peonies, flanked on one side by C. Z. Martin, selling a variety of cheeses and on the other side by Mary Shreiner, selling her wares. Mother usually brought some candy home on market day.

The dairy cows supplied a good portion of the family support. The cows were milked by hand. To cool the milk, we put the milk cans in a trough of cold well water and stirred until it was cold. Emil Strousser picked up the milk daily, then bottled and sold the milk under the name of Rocky Springs Dairy. This small dairy paid the producer a better price per one hundred pound than did the larger dairies.

Mondays were busy days preparing for market. The onions and radishes needed to be pulled, washed and tied into small bunches. The asparagus needed to be weighed and tied into one pound bunches. A few non-producing hens were culled from the flock. Plus a rooster or two were chosen for market. When I was old enough, I was allowed to chop the heads off. I helped to pluck or de-feather them after they were dipped into boiling hot water to loosen the feathers. Then Mother would roll up a few sheets of newspaper and light it with a match to singe the pin feathers and the very fine hairs off the skin. Mother or one of my sisters finished the process of what was called dressing the chicken. At times we would raise a few turkeys and also some capons to be sold on market. I also learned the procedure to caponize a young rooster.

Paul, Bob and me, dressed for church.

I'm not sure about the date of this photo, but it was before Mother had a stroke in 1957.

Seated: Mother and Dad

Standing: Paul, Kathryn (Herr), Bob, Ruth (Siegrist) and Elmer

I attended Millersville Mennonite Church all my life.

CHAPTER FIVE

Early Spiritual Formation

From the time of my birth to today I have regularly attended Millersville Mennonite Church. My spiritual formation began in Sunday school. There was a narrow stairway leading to the basement from the main floor of the church. The classes for children met on benches on one side of the basement. Classes were divided with curtains, not walls. There was a wooden floor under the benches, probably to keep our feet off the cold concrete basement floor. As I remember, Adeliah Leaman was my first teacher in what was called the Card Class. That card showed a Bible scene and a story explaining it. It was about this time the 1927 addition was added to the west end of the church. The addition provided a double stairway to the basement and indoor restrooms, plus more classrooms in the second floor of the annex.

I can think of only one other teacher that I had while I was in the basement, or primary department, as it was called. That was Mary Shertzer. She was a kind lady with a winsome smile and she was a good teacher. She had a daughter with whom I exchanged smiles for a while. It was around that time I was allowed to make a change that I thought was overdue. I was finally allowed to put the knickers aside and wear long pants instead. Clyde Shenk, a young man about 10 years my senior, noticed the change. He had a way to make a young guy feel good. It was also around that time I sensed I was ready for another change. I was giving some serious thought to some of the teaching I heard along the way.

I, too, was a sinner, in need of a Savior. Yes, it was an evangelist, Amos Horst, who gave the altar call, and I responded to the call of the Lord. After a series of instruction meetings, I, along with some others, was baptized, having confessed our faith in Jesus. And we were accepted into and became members of the church.

About that time our Sunday school class was divided, the boys from the girls, and moved upstairs to the main auditorium. It was crowded, with only a few empty benches between the class groups. There were no curtains dividing the classes in the auditorium. One could sometimes find we were listening to a neighboring teacher. Harry Warfel taught our class, and while I was part of this class I was asked to teach a class of young boys. From that time until I was over 80 years old, I served as Sunday school superintendent or as teacher of a class almost every Sunday.

Sunday school superintendents were carefully selected by the ministers. They were pretty careful to select only a man who dressed according to the approved code of the day, meaning one who wore, or was willing to wear the plain coat. Superintendents started their responsibilities as assistant in the primary department for two years, followed by a two-year term as head of the primary department. Next came two years as assistant in the adult department, and then two years as head superintendent. The superintendents were responsible for selecting and recruiting teachers for all the Sunday school classes. Each Sunday, the superintendent opened the Sunday school session with scripture reading and prayer and an introduction to the lesson. At the close of the session, the superintendent led everyone in a review of the lesson and closed with prayer.

In the late 1940s, Weaver Reitz and I were asked to organize and give leadership to what was called the Christian Worker's Band. This was the first time the congregation had an organization especially for the young people. Weaver and I were both already married, with children, but it was typical for young married men to be tapped to lead the youth group. Herbert Fisher was a young pastor at the time, and he was the encourager for this work.

The Christian Worker's Band planned and conducted "cottage meetings" for "shut ins"--people who were not able to attend church services. A typical cottage meeting included scripture reading, a meditation, prayer and singing. Only the young men served as speakers; the girls were allowed to read scripture and poems, but not to give the meditation or lead singing. As I remember it, there were usually 20 or more teenage girls and boys, and also some young singles and other adults who were especially interested in this kind of outreach who participated in the work. We also held street meetings on some Sunday afternoons in Palo Alto, a small town in the coal regions of eastern Pennsylvania.

Another big project for the youth group was taking care of The Lord's Acre, a plot of ground next to the cemetery, where we planted sweet potatoes. Profits from the crop went to Mennonite Central Committee. We also contributed to a fund to purchase a new car for our pastor, Jacob Hess.

After I served eight years as Sunday school superintendent I began teaching the class for the oldest women in the congregation. We met on the short benches at the front corner of the auditorium – in the "Amen" corner. Someone passed on to me some words of appreciation from one of those older women: "Elmer is a good teacher, but I can't hear what he says." Perhaps she was referring to eye contact.

I helped replace the church roof with asbestos slate shingles in the 1950s. The roof is still sound in 2015.

My first year at Wabank School. I am second from the left in the front row. My sister Ruth is first on the right in the second row. Kathryn is second from the right in the back row, standing next to Mylin Herr, who became her husband.

CHAPTER SIX

School Days

School days began for me when I was five and a half years old in September, 1925. That meant I joined my sisters and a few older neighborhood children on that three quarter mile walk to the Wabank one room school with 8 grades. I learned to know Clayton Brenneman as my only class partner in first grade and Anna Brand as the teacher. In an attempt to get us two boys acquainted she asked us to sit on the floor and roll a ball back and forth between us. But I said, "No." It may have been a defiant no. My reasoning was that I would get my pants dirty. But she told my mother about that one with a good chuckle. Years later she would repeat that story. I did learn that it is best not to say "No" to your teacher. The younger classes sat in the front rows and the older ones in back.

Blackboards lined the front of the room, with the alphabet in both small letters and capital letters spread across the top. There was a vestibule on either side in the back, one for the girls and the other for the boys. Here one would have a place for your lunch box, tin cup, coats and boots. Two of the bigger boys carried water from a nearby spring house. The school yard had a flag pole and someone was responsible to raise the flag in the morning and take it down in the evening. A number of trees were there but also enough open space for a ball field. In back of the school we had two outhouses, the kind that had a half moon in the door and a two-seater inside, plus a Sears catalogue to use for paper. One needed permission to go. All you did was snap your fingers to get the teacher's attention, then raise a hand and raise one finger if this was to be a short stay, or two fingers for a longer stay. Now this was in the early days of the airplane and if Pete heard one, his hand was surely raised and he could be seen taking a slow walk back the path, with his eyes scanning the sky.

The school day started with Scripture reading and prayer. Mrs. Brand, as we called her, had a way of discipline that commanded respect. If one was caught using swear words, it meant you needed to have your mouth washed out with soapy water. I never tasted soapy water.

Early in our schooling we learned the Palmer method of hand

writing, which meant arm movement rather than just the wrist. We learned to write in cursive from the very beginning, rather than in print, as children do now. I remember walking home from school as a little guy, facing that cold northwest wind. I found refuge by walking back of the biggest and broadest person. We enjoyed those fifteen minute recess periods and the longer lunch hours. It gave time to play various games, such as softball, touch tag football, collie-over and prisoner's base. One felt accomplished when you could be the first one to say "144" when asked what is 12 x 12, or to say "Tallahassee," when asked to name the capitol of Florida.

The holiday season gave reason for school plays or dramas. Dickens' Christmas Carol brings to mind hearing Mylin Herr say, "Ba, Humbug" representing Scrooge in his frosty voice. I was asked to represent "Old King Cole" one year. Do you remember that little jingle? "Old King Cole was a merry old soul, and a merry old soul was he..." It was around this time that I had an occasion to stop by the Eshbach farm and they were pouring a cement walk. Now this may have been the first time that I had seen soft cement and I made the comment that it looks like "smutz." Well those guys wanted to get some mileage out of that one, and they called me "King Smutz." That was a name that stayed with me for a number of years. I thought it had died until one day, sixty-some years later, a man approached me. After introducing himself as Clayton Brenneman, he paused and with a big grin on his face said, "King Smutz!" Now that was time for a good belly laugh. He had moved into our area and noticed my name on the mailbox. You see, Clayton and I were classmates the first few years of school.

A few more memories come to mind, such as how we gathered around those floor registers to warm our feet. And those pumpkin pies that we enjoyed over Thanksgiving. There was one exception; that girl that dressed a little slovenly and spit the grape skins on the floor. Somehow the pie that came from that home didn't make a hit. On Fastnacht Day donuts were in good supply, thanks to Lizzie Keagy. Valentine's Day! That meant an exchange of valentines using the number code to give identity. The letter C was # 3 and a D was #4, etc. Each Friday, before dismissal time, the upper grades were expected to give a quote that had a hidden meaning. Example: "The mill will never grind with the water that has passed." This means that a lost opportunity is gone forever.

Boarding the bus bound for West End Avenue School, which later became James Buchanan School in Lancaster Township.

It was at this time that the schools in Lancaster Township were consolidating. The Wabank School was sold and became a residence. The next September we boarded a Larabe 6 (six cylinder) bus to what was then called the South West End Avenue School, for grades one through nine. This school bordered the city, but was part of Lancaster Township. I was a bit younger than many of my classmates, so this transition to a large school seemed to be the time to repeat sixth grade. The transition went well. Paul and I soon made new friends, many of whom did not have the rural background.

The next step was entering junior high school where I had more new experiences. In physical ed. or gym classes, no one wanted to be last out of the shower room because that's the one that got swished with a towel by the gym teacher. We also got introduced to the wood shop, using the various saws, the wood lathes, some metal work, mechanical drawing and other new things.

My friend John Schock and I work in the shop at Manor Township High.

47

There were also the track teams, both junior and senior varsity teams. We learned the value of team efforts. It was on that senior track team that I lettered for the four hundred yard relay race and the running broad jump.

The wood shop took my greatest interest. With my teacher's permission, I would stay after school to work in the shop and hitch-hike a ride home. Or sometimes the teacher, Stanley Golden, would take me home in his 1930 Ford.

As I was approaching graduation time from junior high  school the principal of the school, Elizabeth R Martin, stood by my desk and asked me if I was considering going to high school. I do not remember my reply, but she said, "I think you should, Elmer. You ask good questions." Maybe that was all the encouragement I needed. I remember Miss Martin now when I drive by the school building that carries her name on Wabank Road, just below where I grew up.

I enrolled as a sophomore at Manor Township High that fall, after giving Dad my promise to help with fall farm work and go to school on rainy days. So that meant I missed most of the first six weeks of school. The fact that we did not live in Manor Township meant that we did not have bus service. Many times I walked the mile and a half to the high school and other times I was picked up by other commuters.

I chose the agriculture courses. We had classes on animal husbandry, farm accounting

I borrowed a suit coat from my friend John Schock for my senior picture.

and shop. Shop class was divided into time periods of electrical, metal and wood working. I also had social studies and biology. I was a member of the Future Farmers of America (FFA) Club, where I served as treasurer a couple years and as president in my senior year. The FFA motto was "We learn to do by doing." That motto served me well over the years.

I was again intrigued by the wood shop experience. By the end of my senior year I had made a walnut library table that graced our home. It is now cherished by our daughter in their home. My teacher, Howard Siglin, gets a lot of credit for

Ready to graduate
from Manor Township
High, Millersville, PA
May, 1938

teaching me basic woodworking skills. He is also the one that gifted me with that good hunting dog, Penny, that I spoke of earlier. I yearned to try out for the varsity baseball and basketball teams, but my parents had reasons to say no to that one. They didn't want me to spend the extra time away from home. I did participate in a school play.

May 20, 1938 was the date when 69 students received our long anticipated diplomas. Right after graduation we headed off for a three day trip to Washington D.C. followed by a bitter sweet separation. Our first class reunion was fifty years later. How we did enjoy that one!

I got some hands-on experience in carpentry at home by putting windows in the end of our shed, enlarging the hen house on the farm, and building a brooder house in which to start baby chicks.

Learning a trade

Early in 1940 I started serving as an apprentice carpenter with Harry Foutz, a local builder. I started at thirty cents per hour. Being an apprentice, I had a lot to learn. I was helping to nail siding on the side of a barn as the boss came on the scene. He said to me, "No cat faces up there." He was telling me to hit the nail square on the head and do not put a dent in the board. Now the word 'square' could mean a tool used to make a straight line on a board to cut it to length; or the framing square, used to cut rafters, or stair horses. It was important to know how to sharpen a cross cut saw and a rip saw. It was important to know how to use a plumb bob, and how to read blue prints and to make sure that the foundation is square. I needed to learn how to handle height and to be comfortable when walking a narrow rail. After a few months my wages jumped to 35 cents per hour.

I did learn to handle height. In fact, in 1958, when a heavy snow storm collapsed Ben Shertzer's barn roof, I helped with the barn raising. Head carpenter, Christ Ebersole, asked for a volunteer to spike the rafters at the peak of the roof. I volunteered, and it satisfied a yearning I had to do that job. Not everyone feels comfortable in the thin air up there at the peak of a barn roof, and word kind of gets around about who did it. Marty Lefever also volunteered, and he started at the east end and I started at the west end of the roof. That yearning was satisfied and I never had to do it again – "been there, done that," I guess.

As an apprentice my job assignments were varied. Turning the boring machine was assigned to the apprentice boy. Charles Eshelman had the timbers marked where the mortises should be made. It was my job to cut the mortises by boring three or four holes, squaring them up with a chisel and making sure I followed the lines.

Now, a good carpenter takes pride in his work. As Charles Eshelman and I were driving home one day, going by the Millersville Mennonite Church, he said, "Take a look at how straight that roof line is." He had helped build the church some years earlier. Those two years gave me some varied experiences in both repair and new building assignments. I think I could have framed a barn or finished the trim work on a house, but the other guys could do it faster. It was then that I turned my interests back to farming and dating.

The library table I made in high school, now used in our daughter
Norma Jean's home.

My dad, brothers, and I started farming on Charlestown Road in 1942.

CHAPTER SEVEN

The Farm on Charlestown Road

In the spring of 1942, Dad, my brothers and I, started farming the Manor Township farm that I referred to in another part of this story. This farm was not equipped for dairy in order to sell milk. Soon my carpentering skills helped with building a milk house. Another two-story building needed new siding and I put windows in the upper story of that building to make it a chicken house. We now had room for 15 cows, a stable of steers and a horse. We milked cows by hand in those days, and Omer Charles helped with the milking. The barn had been destroyed in 1938 by fire, so we had a new barn. It was equipped for hanging six acres of tobacco. There was also a tobacco shed large enough for three acres, a hog pen, plus another small chicken house.

In 1941 Dad bought his first tractor, a small John Deere H.

So, with the help of Omer Charles and family, who lived in the house, we started the operation. We needed another tractor and purchased a 1943 John Deere B. This had steel wheels because of the war.

Many Lancaster County farms were bought with tobacco money and little thought was given to it. But the time came when I was hearing comments about the use of tobacco. I was told by several men, "Never start the habit; I wish I would not have started." My dad stopped chewing tobacco and he did not want his boys using it in any form, even though we were growing it. I found this too inconsistent to my way of thinking. My mind was drawn to a phrase of scripture found in Romans 14:22, "Blessed is the man who does not condemn himself by that which he approves." Another word for blessed is happy. I remember a conversation with Dad about this issue.

I told Dad that I can plant a field of wheat and ask God's blessing on it, but I cannot do it on the tobacco. I also knew that Dad was counting on the money made on this farm to help purchase another farm for my brother. We met at the bargaining table. We agreed that I could have two acres to grow another crop and receive all the profit, if the tobacco acreage was reduced by two acres. I agreed to help with the tobacco, but would not receive any money from it for a short time.

It was about this time that a drug company was contracting

farmers to grow belladonna. From this plant they produced a medicine. To describe the plant, I would say it is a multi-stemmed plant with bell-shaped leaves. At harvest time the stems were tied onto a lath and hung in the shed to dry, using charcoal as a source of heat. This was a rather lucrative venture. After two years the drug company decided to move to another area, so that opportunity was gone.

We turned this tobacco shed into a chicken house in 1957.

Ready to roll in my new 1938 Dodge, my first car.

CHAPTER EIGHT

Dating—Finding "Miss Right"

I was now eighteen, a high school graduate. My parents had given me a new 1938 Dodge sedan as payment for my services on the farm. Was I ready for dating?

I should note also that being a Christian, I desired to seek the same. After a few dates with my first date we called it off. A friend encouraged me to date another girl and so I did. A customary practice at that time was to take your date to church somewhere nearby. Another one was double or triple dating.

And so it was that one night four of us squeezed in the back seat of a car, and it was tight. Should I or should I not put my arm around her to add to our comfort? Well I did. And I also remember that she took hold of my hand and held it firmly, not wanting me to explore the near parts of her body. At least that was my take on that one. I was learning.

There was concern amongst the ministry that young men receive teaching on Christian courtship and marriage. Teaching sessions were planned, usually on a Sunday afternoon at some church in the county. This was well accepted. These teachers could talk from experience. They too had been young and knew the power of the sex drive, and how impulsive it can be. The thrust seemed to be to set goals; boundary lines that one will not pass over.

Now I think of a day when I was somewhere in my teens and working side by side with my father (Dad, as we called him) in the tobacco field. In my mind I could almost walk to the spot. The field was north of the barn and east a short way. We talked as we worked and I think it was Dad who brought up the subject of the last Sunday's Sunday school lesson. It was about Joseph and Potiphar's wife (Genesis 39). The story tells us that Potiphar's wife saw Joseph as a handsome young man and wanted him to go to bed with her. But Joseph had a ready answer for her. "How could I do such a wicked sin against God?" I think Dad was giving me a lesson on pure living.

Getting back to where I said I was learning. Well, I learned that this girl that I was dating had another suitor, and I moved on. Not willing to be deterred or discouraged, I became acquainted with another Christian girl. It was here that

I dropped anchor, so to speak. We enjoyed each other's company and also the time we spent with many other dating couples.

Week followed week and soon a year passed as time moved on and on. Shall I be blunt and tell you a hand that once restrained was not there? The kiss and tight embrace seemed to be accepted and enjoyed as time moved on until one Sunday night she expressed thoughts of breaking the relationship, and we did. But I did return the next night for some further discussion and resolve. So we parted, both remaining virgins. I pulled up my anchor and left.

I was now some months over twenty years of age and free. As I was leaving home one evening I lit up my first cigarette and it was my last. That day there was another resolution added to my growing list. Before I started dating another girl it seemed important to me that another resolution was added. I had already resolved that I would not take a first drink of alcohol. Now I further resolved that I will not kiss another girl until the engagement kiss. "So help me, Father." My prayer closets seemed to be my bedroom, a remote area back of the barn or by the feed chest in the barn. The quest was on and I was looking for "Miss Right."

In the months that followed I dated several nice girls and one that I thought maybe I should spend more time with. This went on for some time, until one night I asked her a question.

This was not a premeditated question but a bold one. "Is there anything about you that I should know?" The answer was "Yes." Then a pause. I will put it in my words. She had lost her virginity and he fled. Yes, this transgression can be forgiven, but the scar remains. Having that information, I too fled with a saddened heart. "Thank you, Father."

Time brings changes, and new faces become available. And so it was that one Saturday night a friend pointed one out to me. "That's Ruth Garber over there." And she did not have a date. Now I had known several guys that had spent some time with a Ruth Garber. I also learned that she had just returned from a short term of Bible study at Eastern Mennonite College in Harrisonburg, VA. My mind was racing. I reasoned that was why she did not have a date. It was time to make a move. Not that night, but soon. But I had a problem. I did not know where she lived. The problem was solved when a distant cousin of hers said, "I will take you to her home."

Not finding her at home that afternoon, I returned in the evening and we met at the front door. After I introduced myself I asked her if she had plans for the evening. Her response was yes, she was asked to take charge of children's meeting that night at one of the city churches. I volunteered my services to take her there. But Ruth then said that her sister and cousin and Edith Herr were planning to go along also. Well the two girls sensed the situation and they declined to go with her. But Ruth said, "I cannot disappoint Edith." So we picked up Edith at a neighboring farm and we three went to church that night. That night I learned two things about Ruth. She handled the children's class well and she was compassionate in her relationship with Edith. And so we started our relationship on March 8, 1942.

We were in the midst of World War II. Many young men were drafted and some women enlisted. The government did recognize and grant a C-O status for those who had a conscientious objection to war. Those with a C-O status served in what was called an alternate service, a given amount of miles away from home. This work included soil conservation, forestry, working in a mental hospital, dairy milk testing, "guinea pigs" in health care and other activities.

The government also granted farm deferments for those that met the required production standards. I went to Harrisburg for a physical, but did not serve in alternate service because I was granted a farm deferment. Food production was considered essential; building new automobiles was not. Many items were rationed, such as gasoline, sugar, tires and the list went on. New tractors were available only on steel wheels.

And so it was in this gas rationed period that I was enjoying getting acquainted with, maybe, "Miss Right." Limited gas meant limited driving, sometimes car pooling, and only one date per week. Sometimes I pedaled those eight miles to her home on bicycle.

The social order that we enjoyed was going to a church service nearby for some special meeting or perhaps an evangelistic meeting. Usually we went where a large number of other young people gathered. Many times after the service we were invited to another couple's house only to find two or three more couples were also there. We enjoyed games together, sometimes singing by the piano, but always there was a treat to eat together. The next week it may happen at another home.

We found our friendship was growing and soon it seemed important to date on Saturday evening also. About this time I was asked by our Deacon at my church, which was Millersville Mennonite Church, to teach a class of young boys in Sunday school. This required study and Ruth and I began to spend time doing it together at times on Saturday nights.

My father had a desire for more land. The 25 acres of our little farm was not enough. Plus his desire was to keep his boys as lovers of the soil. And so on February 16, 1942, my parents signed a deed for a 97 acre Manor Township farm for $21,000. This farm was on the east end of Charlestown Road. There was a large stone house and a fairly new barn, which replaced the barn that burned down several years earlier.

Ruth seems to enjoy relating that, rather early in our courtship, as we happened to drive past that farm, I asked her an innocent question. "What color would look best on those house shutters?" That question may have been a factor leading to what happened on a certain shopping trip months later.

I was enjoying my time with a well disciplined, fun loving lady. There seemed to be a more serious question raised. While both of our parents raised tobacco on their farms and also seemed to forbid its use, there seemed to be a growing conviction among some of us that if it was wrong to use it, it was also wrong to grow it. This issue was cause for concern in relationships.

There was another matter on my mind, too. At this time our church used what is called the "lot" system to choose bishops, ministers or deacons to fill these positions. If a congregation needed a deacon or minister, votes, or nominations, were taken from within the congregation. This could lead to a few men receiving the number of votes (nominations) required. A designated time was set that the men and their wives, if married, received council and also had the privilege to withdraw if not willing to serve. The remaining names were then made known to the congregation. At a set time and day the ordination was to take place. A bishop gave a qualification sermon often using Acts 1:26 to affirm the scriptural method for selecting a minister. The bishop then handed a number of Bibles corresponding to the number of men in the class, along with one slip of paper, the "lot," to two ordained brothers with the instruction to place the paper at a designated place in one of the Bibles. They were to mix them well behind doors and then hand them back to the bishop. The books were again mixed and lined up on a table or the pulpit. After prayer and a hymn which was also a prayer, such as "Have Thine Own Way, Lord" it was time for a decision to be made. Not having any clue where the "lot" had been placed, the oldest, being first, had the choice of any book. And so, according to age, the men selected a Bible until the youngest of the group had to take the one remaining book. Needless to say, these were tense moments. The bishop in charge then opened the books, starting with the oldest and moving down the line until the "lot" was found. Then an announcement was made similar to that found in Acts 1:26, "They gave forth their lots and the lot fell upon Matthias and he was numbered with the eleven apostles." In this case the brother was ordained to the ministry.

Saying all of that and the fact that I wanted all the i's dotted and all the t's crossed, I asked Ruth another question. "If the church were to call me to become a minister, would that change our relationship?" Ruth assured me it would not.

(Sure enough, in 1955, it happened. Millersville Mennonite Church needed a minister. As the votes were taken from the congregation, I was one of the six men receiving the required number of votes. Ruth and I gave our consent to serve if called. It was then that the lot fell on Benjamin Eshbach.)

The positives far out-numbered the negatives in our relationship. Had I known what happened on a certain shopping trip earlier that summer, I may have had the courage to pop the real question sooner.

August 28, 1943 became an important date. It was then, in the living room on the New Danville farm, that I asked Ruth Garber to be my wife. The answer came with a very pleasant smile and what I perceived to be a well thought through "Yes!" And this occasion was sealed with a kiss, our very first. It was not the practice among Mennonites to give an engagement ring, but I did give a sizeable Wallace Nutting painting to her as our engagement gift. That picture portrays a meandering stream flowing through a meadow. Some areas are shallow with ripples and other areas are placid and calm. That stream brought a thought to my mind that my Sunday school teacher, Harry Warfel, shared. He likened deep water to deep love. It flows smoothly. Shallow water represents troubled waters. Harry was my Sunday school teacher while I was a teenager until I was asked to teach the class of young boys.

Now back to that night where excitement and joy abounded. Ruth told me later that she wanted to tell her parents about our engagement right away. She was overjoyed to the point that she woke her parents up and shared the news. They too were rejoicing.

All was going well and plans were being made. Extra costs needed to be met. The economy was improving and the Garbers decided to seed a rather large plot of turnips. They found a ready market for the turnips, providing some extra income to help meet the wedding expenses.

Now about that shopping trip: This was top secret stuff; something that even I was not told until many months later. And even now I am hesitant to put in print. But I will. Ruth bought her wedding dress material before she was engaged. White dotted Swiss marquisette. The rationale used? It was war time and nice fabrics were disappearing from the shelves. She and her mother decided to purchase the fabric when they saw it; they couldn't count on finding appropriate fabric just any time. Smart Lady! Then again, maybe that question I so innocently asked about the shutters was a factor.

There was excitement in the air. Plans were being made and then checked off the "to do list" when completed. Things were going so well that I thought I didn't need to ask any more questions. I had never asked Ruth's father if I could have her hand in marriage. I thought it was just in the old days that the young man needed to ask the father for permission to marry his daughter. And then it happened, as Ruth and I started out the lane on our way to the courthouse to apply for our marriage license. There, just beyond the bend, was Ruth's daddy working at something. I had a sense he had something on his mind. I stopped the car and leaned out the window. I simply said "Is this alright?" He answered with a smile and said "Yes." Hindsight tells me I was wrong. The parents' blessing should be sought early.

The day had come. February 19, 1944, and I was told that I did not need to help with the morning chores at home. But I did clean the horse stalls, just to pass the time. The wedding was scheduled for twelve o'clock at the bride's home. Family and friends were gathering in. Stoner Krady, the bishop, was there. My brother, Paul served as best man and Ruth's sister, Marian, served as bride's maid. The clock struck twelve, the men's quartette started singing, "O Father Lead Us" as the bridal party filed in. After a short meditation by Bishop Krady, the vows were exchanged and we became husband and wife.

Shortly thereafter Eli Hostetter, the head chef, announced "Come, the dinner is now ready to serve." About 100 guests enjoyed a great meal at tables set up in all parts of the Garber home. Many congratulations were given and some pictures were taken. Soon it was time to hit the road.

Uh-Oh! Those young guys found the car and did they do a job! We started off, leaving the cans dragging behind us. I am sure it was to their delight. After traveling a few miles we removed the cans before we entered the city of Lancaster, and we also prayed. I am sure it was a prayer of thanks and a request to the Lord to lead us on!

While there were two of us in the car, I was the only one that knew where we were going. So I took the lead, I mean the wheel, and we started on our way. We had only a half tank of gas. Surely that would take us to the next county and home again.

In due time, we were standing by the registration desk in the famous Hershey Hotel. Yes, they were expecting us. When we got off the elevator and walked down the hall to our room, two ladies came by and sensing who was approaching, they started singing "Here comes the bride, please step aside." How nice. How good it felt that we were married! Our families and friends seemed to enjoy the day. It was great. Yes, here we were, starting life's journey together. This was an unchartered journey. We had not traveled this way before. We were so glad that we had a Captain that knew the way.

As I reflect on our wedding day I can also reflect with joy on celebrating our 70th wedding anniversary. We are still kissing. As I think back to those dating days, my Captain was using people to direct me. I remember my mother's admonition "Be good, Elmer" as I passed through the kitchen door; my dad, as we worked together on the farm; my older sisters and my younger brothers, who may have been taking some cues from me; certainly the teaching I received from Sunday school teachers, from pastors, and those meetings for young men. They were all helping me to chart the way. All I needed to do was follow. As we left the hotel the next morning we were rejoicing. We were husband and wife. No need to scan the crowd. The searching was over. That time was past.

> Great it is to believe the Dream
>
> When we stand in youth,
>
> Beside the Starry Stream
>
> But it's a greater thing to fight life through,
>
> And say at the end
>
> "The Dream was True."
>
> -Markham

That day we traveled to the nearby town of Palmyra where we worshiped with our good friends, John and Ruth Schock. We had dinner and a visit with them and then we moved on to the next nearby town of Annville to visit my cousin Mabel and her husband, Marlin Weaver. We had accepted their invitation to stay a few days with them. They treated us royally and I remember most vividly what happened the first night we were there. They thought we needed some more excitement in our lives and they had a plan. As we were snuggled in bed that first night and all was quieted down, suddenly a loud noise came from under the bed. Soon we found a vacuum cleaner under the bed with the cord reaching under the door and into the hall. Yes, Mabel, it worked! By mid week we were home and yes, the gas reached.

The day after our wedding we went to church with my buddy from high school, John Schock and his wife Ruth, then visited in their home before heading to the next town to visit my cousin.

Part Two

Ruth Writes

Daddy's parents
Simon and Fannie Eby Garber

Mother's parents,
Harry and Susan Shenk Herr

Here I am at age nine months.

My parents, J Clarence Garber
and E Vera Herr Garber when
they got married, in 1922

CHAPTER NINE

Who Am I?

I was the firstborn in the family. On January 8, 1923, mother was already in the Lancaster General Hospital. She had albumin (extra protein) in her urine during the last week and needed a special procedure for this condition and lots of precaution, so she unexpectedly needed to be hospitalized a week before I was born. Daddy realized the gravity of the situation and there was lots of rejoicing when God answered their prayers and a healthy 7-pound baby girl was born at 6 o'clock in the evening. They named me Ruth, just because Mother liked that name.

My sister Marian was born two years later on May 23, 1925. She married Henry B. Leaman and they lived on Windy Hill Road on the east side of Lancaster, PA. Our next sister was named Anna Martha after her two great aunts. She was born

February 16, 1927. She was a nurse who lived near the places she worked as an RN. The fourth girl, Vera Jean, was born two years later on February 13, 1929. She became a nurse midwife and later married John Huang who was from Taiwan and they lived in Baltimore, MD.

We four girls enjoyed being little girls together. We especially played with dolls and had lots of tea parties. We played church and school. When Jean was about three years old I remember a salesman came to the gate and saw us little girls playing in the yard. He asked "Where are the boys?" "Oh," I answered, "don't you know this is a girl farm?" On February 2, 1933, a baby brother, Jay Clarence, joined the family. This was a very exciting event. Jay, as we called him, was a treasure, ten years younger than I was.

Jay was a gentle young child. He enjoyed playing with my doll coach on the cement walk that ran across our lawn. He pushed it so fast that it almost fell apart. When he was about six years old he carried some small stones into the kitchen and threw them at his sisters because he didn't like something they did to him. I remember taking him aside and explaining to him that girls don't appreciate the rough ways boys have in physically hurting them at school and other places. I really feel he got the point. I never saw him to be mean to anyone from that time to his adult years.

My mother, Vera Herr Garber, cared a lot about our past. She had the desire to pass on to her grandchildren the colorful stories belonging to her relatives, including her father and mother. Her foresight as well as her appreciation for her heritage was recorded in her first book entitled, "The Beaten Path of Papa and His Folks." With some encouragement from her family she wrote her second book "Capturing 60 Years as a Farmer's Wife" after she turned 80 years of age. Both books are treasures for the family. This book, my story, is a sequel for our family.

As I start writing about my life's story I begin with my interpretation of who my parents and grandparents were and how they affected my character and personality.

My father, J. Clarence Garber, was born June 1, 1898, the fifth child in a family of seven. The Garber family was raised on a farm in West Donegal Township, near Elizabethtown, in northwestern Lancaster County, PA. Today West Donegal Township is still a quiet farming area that has not seen much change as one compares it to many areas of Lancaster County.

Daddy's parents were Simon and Fannie Eby Garber. As long as I can remember my Grandpa Garber was a preacher at the Bossler Mennonite Church. They lived about a mile from the farm where I spent my childhood. They had a new house with a grape arbor over the front of the porch. One time Grandma invited my cousin, Peggy Garber, and me over for a tea party. She also invited two children about our ages who were visiting grandparents in the neighborhood. She set up a nice card table under the grape arbor, which was one step off the porch. She served us graham crackers with some of her homemade applesauce on them. She made us feel very special. At least I did.

Inside the porch door there was a round dining room table. Standing in the middle of the table was a beautiful tiffany lamp. The light shone on the reading material that Grandpa was reading. We frequently saw him reading his Bible. He would generally move his lips as he silently read the words. In church he spoke deliberately, and meaningfully related each special story or event. I loved hearing him because he didn't preach so long and it seemed to have meaning for a young 8 to 12 year old girl like I was.

My Grandma Garber was a good cook. She especially made good chicken corn soup for our family gatherings. She and Grandpa had a neat garden back of the house. Grandpa made raised beds with boards along the paths where the lettuce, spinach, onions, strawberries, sugar peas and string beans each had their bed. I loved to walk those paths and have Grandma show me how everything was growing just right.

There were some currant bushes and gooseberry bushes around the edges of the garden. Grandma made jelly and pies from those berries. She sent me to the corner cupboard upstairs in the bathroom at times to get a jar of jelly. Each jar was labeled. We spread those homemade jams and jellies on our bread.

Sometimes Grandpa would ask us if we wanted a piece of sugar bread. He first put butter on the bread and then sprinkled some white sugar all over it. That was a treat I never received from anyone else. Daddy said one time that Grandpa never gave him sugar bread. I guess that was just for his little sweeties.

Grandpa Garber had his 25 or more laying hens in the chicken yard behind his little barn. I enjoyed seeing him scatter some corn out there on the ground and the little flock would rush around like children with a peanut scramble. These in turn kept Grandma supplied with eggs for their breakfasts and the puddings and baked things she made. She often made red beet eggs and deviled eggs as well. The red beet eggs were hard boiled eggs marinated in sweet sour syrup made from the water in which the red beets had been cooked. For deviled eggs she mashed the yolks and mixed in some mustard, mayonnaise and vinegar, and filled the hard-cooked whites.

Grandma made dried apple snitz (small slices) from the Smokehouse variety of apples that grew on their tree behind the house. She dried them on the radiator beside the kitchen table. I remember when they bought their first electric refrigerator. It stood beside their kitchen table. Grandma was a thrifty housekeeper. She didn't waste anything. She explained to us that she always set everything that was to go into the refrigerator on the table nearby and then quickly put it all in as she opened the door just one time after a meal.

When Grandma Garber washed the grains of rice for rice pudding she assured me she didn't let one grain get lost in the sink. When she came to our farm orchard she thought it would be a sin to let any "drops" rot away. So she picked them up regularly and made applesauce or dried them. She used all the left over dress fabrics from her sewing cupboard to make the nicest quilt patches. She was an excellent quilter and she also made many buttonholes by hand for the garments made by the sewing circle at the church.

Grandma had white hair tucked up in her white prayer veiling with black ribbon ties that were neatly tied under her chin most of the time. She wore a cape that had two points and opened down the front over the top of her dress. She wore an apron of the same material, which she tied around Grandma had white hair tucked up in her white prayer veiling with black ribbon ties that were neatly tied under her chin most of the time. She wore a cape that had two points and opened down the front over the top of her dress. She wore an apron of the same material, which she tied around her waist for church and other occasions. This was required of the preachers' wives in those days. Someone told me the apron covered the pregnant woman's growth and her dress could be adjusted easily under the apron. Her "everyday" dress had an apron, possibly of a different cotton fabric, that had a bib pinned at her chest with black-headed straight pins.

Grandma Garber was available to care for my sisters and me while my parents went away for a short time. Invariably she would have time to sit on her little rocking chair, which she used for hand sewing. She would ask us to comb her long hair. Each one took a turn. The first one had the privilege to take out the hairpins. They were not wire but instead were called bone. They were tan or dark brown in color. Her long white hair hung back over the chair and reached almost to her waist. We took her heavy ivory colored comb and ran it from her forehead to her waist. Sometimes she reminded us to "comb a little harder." Our turns lasted from five to 10 minutes. The last one tried to put her hair in a bun on top of her head and place those five or six hairpins in properly. How we would laugh when the hair would unwind again. We had a difficult time trying to get Grandma to look right again. After we all finished taking our turns, Grandma would go to her bookcase desk, open the drawer and get out her little coin purse. She paid us each a penny for combing her hair. That was another penny for our little banks at home. We felt well paid. Some of my cousins have the same memories of combing Grandma's hair.

Grandpa Simon Garber was a rather large man. He had the reputation of "sitting all over the seat." He came to the farm to do odd jobs for my daddy. I remember following him as he used the big scythe to cut off the weeds around the barn. I remember going for a walk with him in the pasture. As we came to a "cow pie" he said to me, "Don't tramp the blind man's eye out. He can't see you coming." In other words "don't tramp in the cow pie."

My Grandpa and Grandma Herr, Harry and Sue, lived 25 miles away, near New Danville, south of Lancaster, PA. It was a big trip for us to go to visit them. When we arrived at their door there was usually a receiving line waiting to shake hands with us. First it was Grandpa, then his brother Uncle Ira and his wife, Aunt Anna, who lived in Millersville. Next was Aunt Martha, who lived with Grandpas in their house. Then there was Grandma who also shook our hands. Aunt Martha and Aunt Anna were Grandma's sisters. Sometimes Aunt Martha's husband, Uncle Mart Nissley was in the line also. He lived in Mechanicsburg, PA. Uncle Mart was a businessman who bought potatoes from farmers. He had a "housekeeper" at his apartment in Mechanicsburg. Aunt Martha rarely visited that apartment. These folks were all glad to see us and collectively they had a large meal ready when we arrived.

One of my favorite foods was the tapioca pudding Grandma Herr made and served in a large blue and white serving dish made in Germany. I enjoy using that same dish to serve tapioca pudding today, even at church dinners. Grandpa Herr loved to garden and his pride and joy was his sweet corn which he always pulled off at just the right stage to make the best roasting ears, with lots of butter and salt spread on them. Grandpa was proud of his fine Stayman Winesap apples and the arch cellar under the hill smelled so sweet when he opened its door to give us a sample of the apples.

As this meal was being prepared, Grandpa, Aunt Martha and sometimes Uncle Mart would help Grandma by giving suggestions about how to make everything taste the best. When serving pig stomach, some thought you jag it with a fork while baking and others thought that would let out the tasty juices. Anyway, the potato, sausage and bread filling used to stuff the pig stomach always proved to be a treat as it was sliced and served with pride.

I was five or six years old when mother helped me memorize a poem about a little girl. Mother wanted me to recite the poem when we visited Grandpa and Grandma Herr and the other great aunts one Sunday. I did not want to recite this that day. Mother took me into the next room and lovingly coaxed me, "Please say your poem. They will enjoy hearing you so much." So I finally agreed as follows:

"The Little Girl Who Won't Recite"

I know my ABC's and I know Black Bird baked into a pie

And lots of songs that I can sing;

Of course, I don't know everything.

But since I'm only half past three, I think I know enough for me.

I know Miss Muffet and Boy Blue and yes, I know Jack Horner too;

And Simple Simon and sometimes I go through all my nursery rhymes;

But never when there's company, I won't tell

---

strangers all I know.

Sometimes they say, "Now won't you please stand up and speak your ABC's?"

But I just hang my head and say, "No, I don't want to. Not today."

And Mother says, "It bothers me to see how stubborn she can be;

Why almost all day long she sings

and says so many pretty things."

And then they say: "Well never mind; some other little girl we'll find,

Who'll speak her pieces and not stare forever at the carpet there."

I like to say my pieces when the company has gone again;

But when the're sitting all about, the words I know just won't come out.

On Mother's lap, my face I hide and I get all mixed up inside.

Edgar Guest--1926

Everyone smiled and enjoyed my recitation, perhaps especially because the poem so nearly reflected our exact situation that day.

My mother, Emma Vera Herr, (she didn't care for the name Emma, so she used E. Vera as her name) grew up in that home, where there were always extra relatives living with them in the large brick farm house along the New Danville Pike. Her grandparents, Martin B. and Annie Shenk Herr and

Great Uncle Jake Shenk, who was Grandma Herr's mother's brother, and Aunt Martha who was Grandma Herr's sister, all had ideas of how the children should be raised. Mother was the oldest, born on April 13, 1898. She was named Vera because Grandpa read a book in which Vera was the main character and he liked that name. Mother was a submissive, charming little girl, very much loved by her Grandpa from what I gathered in her stories.

Her brother, Elvin, was the young man and became the farmer. He never cared for the orchard as much as his father did. Uncle Elvin married Elizabeth (Betty) Witmer, from Lampeter. He served as deacon at the New Danville Mennonite Church, and many years later, spearheaded efforts to restore the historic Hans Herr property. Both of my grandparents, Harry and Sue, were eighth generation descendents of Hans Herr.

Elizabeth was the youngest child. I always admired the way she decorated her house and landscaped her big lawn. She was orderly and her three children were well behaved. Aunt Betty's husband was Harry Houser, from Willow Street, PA.

In contrast, my mother was a dreamer. She dreamed about marriage. She told me that as a young girl she thought, "If I ever have a husband and a kitchen cabinet, I will be satisfied." The tramps, the men who would ask to stay in the barn as they traveled through the countryside, fascinated her when she was a young girl. The men would many times fix up their living quarters in the granary on the second floor in Grandpa's barn. Mother would sneak a look around and envy them, living there so simply in the barn.

Mother's folks did everything on the right day, the right week and the right season. They did the spring housecleaning, beating the carpets, polishing the tin ware and scrubbing the porch, at just the right time. Mother's personality did not accept this time line and she just wanted to live and let live. She wanted to do fine embroidery work, read poetry and see the wonders of God's creation. As a young mother, she loved her babies and dreamed of who they would become some day. For her, keeping house took second place after her other interests. She said, "At least I know how it ought to look."

When Mother was 90 years old I periodically had the privilege of being with her in the exercise pool at the Mennonite Home. She enjoyed those times and we would many times sing songs as we basked in the comfort of the warm water while doing some light exercises. One of her songs was a memory from her early years. I do not have the tune, but the words reveal the note of a dreamer, as I mentioned she was:

> "With someone like you, a pal good and true,
>
> I'd like to leave it all behind and go and find
>
> Some place that's known to God alone—Just a spot to call our own;

We'd find perfect peace, where joys never cease,

Out there beneath the kindly sky;

And we'd build a sweet little nest, somewhere in the west,

And let the rest of the world go by."

My daddy, J. Clarence Garber, was number five in a family of seven children. His brother, Henry, who married Ada Nissley, was followed by Norman, who married Belle Kauffman, and Aunt Suie was married to Martin Kraybill. Uncle John was next. He married Anna Houser, who was from York County. Of course, Grandma was wishing for another girl when Clarence was born. But he was a real boy with lots of energy. His brother Monroe followed him and he married Blanche Kauffman. His sister, Helen, who married Earl Groff, completed the family.

Clarence courted my mother, Vera Herr, for a couple years, driving the 25 miles from Elizabethtown to New Danville in his Scripps Booth car once a week. He enjoyed the chocolate cake and English walnuts with which she treated him before he returned home that night. He had graduated from Maytown High School and took a term of college work at Millersville Normal School in order to teach school. He taught the upper elementary grades at the Silver Springs Consolidated school near Marietta, PA. When he and mother got married, January 12, 1922, they used all the money he saved to go to Bermuda, via ship, on their wedding trip. They thoroughly enjoyed that 10-day trip, and Daddy said they decided after they got home that they would never look back and say they wish they would not have spent that money even if it did take their last cent.

I don't remember this car—the one Daddy drove when he courted Mother.

By springtime they moved to the Garber homestead at the "Bossler Corner," about half-way between Elizabethtown and Maytown along what is now called Bossler Road. Grandpa and Grandma Garber moved to a new house about one mile away, with their two youngest children, Uncle Monroe and Aunt Helen. My parents occupied the old farm house in a long lane on 83 acres. This house had no indoor bathroom. Mother explained to me that she had saved enough money to buy a new living room suite for their home. However, Mother had been used to having an indoor bathroom and she asked Grandpa Garber if they could have a bathroom installed if she used her money to pay for it. As a result there was a partition and bathroom fixtures, along with running water installed upstairs to give them the modern convenience of an indoor bathroom. (I understand mother was reimbursed for that sacrifice many years later).

My father was a likable person. He always found something to say to everyone he met. He could judge if people had a good character or if they were not fair or doing a good job. He expected the best from everyone. Even his children knew we needed to do our best in order to please him.

My parents when they celebrated their 60th anniversary.

L-R front row: Anna Martha, Daddy (Clarence), Mother (Vera), Jean.
Center row: Lois Garber, Marian,Leaman, Ruth Rohrer
Back row: Jay Garber, Henry Leaman, Elmer Rohrer

My parents in the 1980s

My childhood home in the Bossler Corner, between
Elizabethtown and Maytown.

Marian and I give Jay, Jean and Anna Martha a sled ride
near the spring on the Bossler Corner farm.

CHAPTER TEN

The Long Lane

Some of my earliest memories took place in the long lane we used to get to our farm buildings from the stony township road that ran between other farms that also had long lanes.

My parents recounted the following story many times. They could not find me one balmy afternoon. In fact, they looked everywhere, all around the house, up in the barn, in the orchard. They may have received a phone call from the neighbor, saying I was at their house. I was three years old and walked all the way out that ¼ mi. long, stony lane. I crossed the road and went to the neighbor's door. We had not visited with those folks. They were the tenant farmer family for the neighbor down the lane across the road from our lane. I can remember one of the grown-up ladies holding me in her arms when my anxious-looking parents came in the door. A big fuss was made about me walking so far by myself and not being at all worked up about it. I remember the feeling of meeting nice, new people in a different house and then having my parents so happy to find me all safe and comfortable. Yes, they wanted me with them. I was important to them.

One of the memorable things that happened to me took place in that long lane. Our mailbox was at the end of the lane and someone always needed to walk out there about noontime each day to get the mail. I was about six years old, as I remember, when I got to the mailbox and saw a brown box about a foot square there on the shelf beside the mailbox. Somehow I thought it looked like my name on the box. I walked in the lane as fast as I could, carrying the newspaper,

a couple letters and the box. The box felt rather heavy and I could shake it a little. As I saw my parents open the box there was a lot of excelsior, something like rough straw, in the box around a baby doll. Daddy said, "Ruth, this is a new dolly for you from Uncle Kelton!" I remember the disbelief and excitement I felt. This baby doll had a china head and soft body with the little legs pulled up. She had tiny fingers and toes on pink little hands and feet. The doll wore a long white dress with a soft pink little sac around its soft body. Oh, what a joyful moment. My small arms cradled this newborn-like doll baby and its eyes went shut with little eyelashes resting on its cheeks.

Uncle Kelton was our "rich uncle" who lived in Boston, Massachusetts. We were not related to him. My parents met him in Bermuda during their honeymoon. Kelton Upham took a special liking to them and kept in touch with our family until he was up in years and died. He was an overweight man with a round, kindly face. One time he came to visit us on the farm. There was some discussion about what chair he would use, on which to place his 300 pounds. A wide wicker chair from the living room was decided upon before he arrived. He never married and he took pleasure in sending us little gifts and cards on our birthdays and at Christmas time. The 5-pound box of mixed chocolates that he sent in the mail for Christmas was the biggest treat of the year for our family. Mother took pleasure in getting out her cutting board and, taking a sharp little knife, she would pick out about five or six of the chocolates and cut them each in four pieces. That way we could each get a little taste of a number of kinds. What a treat that gave us each year! And it arrived in the mailbox at the end of the lane.

One time I was walking in the lane with the mail when a bumblebee started buzzing around my head. Ouch, he stung me on the tip of my nose. I went crying in the lane and Daddy met me near the barn. After telling him what happened, I remember him pulling the stinger out, and then he took some mud from a puddle and laid it on my sting to cool it down. It eventually stopped hurting but I was always very cautious when I passed that spot in the lane. I guess the bumblebees lived near the bushes there on the bank and I didn't want to be stung again.

We had some very heavy snow storms back in those days. There was a large, old bob sleigh back in our barn. After one big snowfall my daddy got out that sleigh and the old horse from the stable. We had a Sunday dinner invitation at the neighboring farm, about two miles away. We could not go there with our car that day so we went on the sleigh. Mother found the old leather strip of sleigh bells to put on the horse's back and after the horse was hitched to the sleigh the seven of us went merrily out the lane and up the hill and down to the tune of jingling bells, to the Christ Miller farm for a great Sunday dinner.

I remember mother driving our Franklin touring car. It had curtains on the windows made of semi-transparent isinglass , instead of glass windows. Isinglass is a form of mica. One day the car stopped as she wanted to go out the lane. It seemed to make her feel badly. As I remember, she cried as we sat there and the car would not go. I wonder now just where she wanted to go or why she had to cry.

The Franklin Touring car had isinglass instead of glass windows. I sat on the floor, covered with blankets when we drove to York in wintertime.

I was the only girl in first grade at Washington School. This picture from the 1929-1930 school term includes some of my cousins. Our teacher was Miss Carrie Smith, on the right end of the second row. She lived with my Grandpa and Grandma Garber. There I am—fourth from the left in the front row.

CHAPTER ELEVEN

School Days

My education started before first grade. Mother read a lot of stories to us. She especially liked the nursery rhymes by Henry Wadsworth Longfellow and poems by James Whitcomb Riley. My imagination was stretched as she read "The Land of Counterpane" and "The Bear Story that Alex 'ist maked up by his-own-se`f" by James Whitcomb Riley, *Little Black Sambo*, *Pollyanna* and *Heidi* were favorites. I remember shedding some tears when she read about Pollyanna sleeping in the attic when her miserable aunt sent her there instead of using one of her many bedrooms.

Mother sat on a sturdy rocking chair with an upholstered seat and no arms on the sides. This chair was always in the dressing room upstairs above the kitchen. We had a dressing room because that was the only room warm enough for changing clothes, especially in the winter. The pipeless furnace in the cellar gave enough hot air to come up through the large, iron register to warm the kitchen and pass on up the smaller register above to warm the dressing room and the little bathroom. Mother sat there rocking babies, doing finger plays and telling us about her childhood days with her cousins.

In that room, when I was almost 10 years old, I remember mother telling me about the birds and the bees and the stamens in the flowers that the bees crawled into for mixing pollen. It didn't make a big impression on me because I was totally surprised when my baby brother was born on Groundhog Day in 1933. Actually, Mother did try to explain where babies came from one day. That evening Daddy and I were in the cow stable and as we were looking at the young heifers, I declared to Daddy, "I know where babies come from." He passed that statement off with, "You do," and then went on talking about the nice heifers in the pen.

I was six and a half years old when one of the young girls at church asked me, "Ruth, do you have a lunch box or are you going to take your lunch in a tut?" I was bewildered. I never heard of a "tut." Yes, I had a lunchbox with a thermos, ready to start school the next day. I walked out the long lane and then another quarter mile with a couple school age children to the Washington one room schoolhouse. It stood beside our church. I had a few new clothes and a pretty little necklace to wear for this big occasion. After I got to school, I discovered not everyone had things alike. Some had book bags. Some of my schoolmates had pretty colored flat lunch boxes, and some used a brown bag – a "tut!" Some had meat in their sandwiches and a nice piece of cake. Others had mostly peanut butter crackers and jelly sandwiches. We were even judged a little by how good our lunches looked. Some had homemade bologna, milk in their thermos and sandwiches wrapped in waxed bread paper. Some brought a shiny apple from the orchard to eat at recess.

Yes, this was when competition started. We had a lady schoolteacher, Miss Carrie Smith. Miss Smith boarded at my Grandpa Garber's home. She seemed to like me a lot. I was the only girl in first grade. There were five boys in the class. I was usually at the head of the class as we stood in a line in the front of the room. We took turns reading a paragraph in our reading book. Sometimes we answered questions and "trapped," or moved ahead of the one beside us if that person did not know the answer.

There were eight grades in this school and the big boys looked like adults to me. We learned to read and write. As we listened to the other grades we gathered some facts and information. The photograph of my first year at Washington School shows there were about 47 students. Miss Smith taught us art and music on Fridays. I remember she helped me draw a poster with large mittens on it.

Miss Smith was my teacher for two years and then she got married. Ladies could not teach after they got married. Mr. John R. Kraybill was my teacher for the next five years. He was a strict disciplinarian. He lost his right hand in a farm accident and therefore had a wooden hand with a black glove over it. He would tap this hand on someone's head now and then, which soon brought order to the classroom. Mr. Kraybill taught us spelling, giving a Milky Way candy bar to anyone who had 25 perfect lessons in a row. We had about 20 words to a lesson. He taught us to diagram sentences. We memorized all the president's names. We stood in the back of the school room and sometimes he would pull maps down in the front of the room. There he would point to European countries and we named them. We memorized the capitol cities of each U.S. state. We memorized "The Village Blacksmith" by Henry W. Longfellow, and "The Wind" by Eugene Field, among other poems.

We played in the large school and church yards, which overlapped. We played "Prisoner's Base" between the side of the school and the side of the church. There was a place where the big children played soft ball. My boy cousins, Wilmer and Simon Kraybill, tried to help me learn to bat the ball. First they gave me a broad board to hit it with. Then they gave me a round bat. That gave the big laugh for the day. No, I was never able to hit the ball very well. We played jump rope, but some girls could jump much longer than I could. I enjoyed playing "London Bridge is Falling Down." After the big snowfalls we pulled our sleds along to school. We used the neighbor's barn hill at recess and lunch hour for fast sled rides that we never forgot.

There were older girls that became my friends. But sometimes they did not accept me. There were days when they seemed to be telling secrets about me, which made me unhappy. When I prayed at night I learned to tell this to God and trust that He would make things go better the next day and they usually did.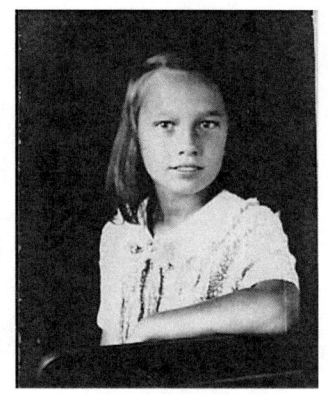

We always had devotions at home before we went to school. Daddy read the scripture passage suggested in the Sunday school quarterly and then we all knelt beside our chair and he would pray the same words each morning. "Thank you for the opportunities of this day. Thank you for our health and strength," and a few other such phrases. Then we would re-peat the Lord's Prayer together out loud. As I got older the words "Forgive us our debts as we forgive our debtors" be-came meaningful to me. I would forgive those girls who were telling secrets about me. I tried to make friends with Mary Alleman, the girl who was less likable or poor, and did special fun things with her instead of depending on friendship with the older girls. That seemed to work.

My sister had some trouble with the same problem and we would talk about this in bed at night. I remember approaching a few of her friends and advising them to not treat others like that. They should love each other at all times. Our cousin, Maribel Kraybill, reminded me many years later that I was the peacemaker for them. I suppose when one is mistreated it helps us sympathize with others going through the same problems and we can realize ways to help in such situations.

The depression years were about over and money became a little more available. My school days were interrupted in the spring of 1936, when my parents made the decision to buy the Herr homestead south of Lancaster. My Uncle Elvin decided to sell the farm and take a salesman's position for the DeKalb corn and chicken business. It was time for my parents to move off the Garber homestead. So on April 1, 1936, a large moving van pulled up to our gate and all the furniture and our belongings were loaded into the van. The cows filled a cattle truck. We had a caravan going those 25 miles to New Danville. As we were leaving the Bossler neighborhood it pulled at the strings in all of our hearts.

Marian and I were the only plain girls at Harmony Hall School, near New Danville. Jean is in the center of the front row, Marian is fifth from the left in the second row, Anna Martha is fourth from the right on the second row, and I am fourth from the right in the third row.

I was finishing the seventh grade. We did not know any of the children in this strange one room school near New Danville, called Harmony Hall. Now we walked out another long lane and up the macadam road called New Danville Pike. A couple cars may have passed us as the four Garber girls walked toward the school that first morning. A few big boys were on the porch watching us walk closer to them. "Here comes the Garbage Family," we heard them say. Evidently they heard a new family was moving into the neighborhood. They had never heard the name Garber. Oh my, in our neighborhood near Elizabethtown the name Garber was well accepted and had some prestige. "The Garbage Family" --no way did that welcome us with any good feelings.

As we walked up the steps to the porch we saw little girls and boys, middle sized and bigger children. We stopped inside and met Miss Harnish, the teacher. My sisters had never had a lady for a teacher. She accepted us warmly and showed us where to put our lunch boxes. There were some nice girls that smiled at us and we were assigned to our desks. It didn't feel too bad, and soon the bell rang for school to begin. The room was much smaller than the Washington School. Less students too, and it felt good to have some girls for each of us to learn to know.

Mr. McKose was the music teacher who came to the school

once a week. My parents learned that he gave private piano lessons as well. I had taken piano lessons at Elizabethtown and now my sisters also started taking lessons. A few years later when I was about 18 years old we four girls played piano quartets and also learned to sing as a quartet.

As the next year came along, Mr. McKose had our school prepare a musical for a Christmas program. It was called, "A Vacation for Santa." Since Mr. Kraybill was a Mennonite Deacon in the church, he never had us learn anything pertaining to Santa or even a Christmas tree. So getting ready for this

Christmas was a new experience for us. To learn a song saying "Santa needs a long va-ca-tion/ Lots of fun and re-creation/ Not to have to crawl/ down a chimney small/ Is a joyful ex-pec-ta-tion. Listen world/to the latest tip/ Captain Claus/ of the Christmas ship/ Soon will be on a good long trip/ For he needs a va-ca-tion." Yes, I remember the words and the tune. And then the play went on with more words and action songs.

I really didn't learn very much in the 8th grade. I missed my old friends at school and church in the Bossler Corner. But the next phase of my education was where I really got stretched. I was 14 years old. It was time to take the test for admittance to high school. I got the letter saying I passed the test. I would need to ride in a bus and go about 8 miles to the Millersville Training School for ninth grade. Go on a bus-- that was something I never did before. The day after Labor Day came. I was scared. My father always said, "This is the way you should do," whenever a new experience was at hand. I didn't know what the bus would look like. He said, "When the bus comes down the road from Conestoga, you wave your arm and let them know you want it to stop for you." So about 7:15 that morning I took my lunch in a tut, a brown paper bag, for the first time. I walked out the long lane to the stone road called Stony Lane, and then out the short distance to the New Danville Pike.

Yes, there it came. Not a yellow school bus, but a large, dark green bus. I did as Daddy said. I waved my arm, as I stood there so tense and scared. Sure enough, the bus stopped. The door opened and the man said, "You get the next bus." He shut the door and off he drove.

I waited again and along came some kind of a vehicle. Is that a bus or what? Yes, it stopped. It looked like a sort of cracker box or crate with windows along both sides. A lady, Mrs. Douts, was the driver. Inside there were a few boys and girls. There were three benches. Two were on the sides facing the center bench that

It wasn't what I expected, but I went to school in Millersville in a bus like this one.

went through the middle. About four or five people could sit on each bench. The bus started off as I sat on the space inside the door. I was glad to see a few friends that I learned to know in eighth grade. We rattled along over the bumps and hills of Long Lane and across the Conestoga River on the wooden covered bridge, and around the corners of Slackwater Road. Finally we reached our destination at the Millersville Training School. This is where the students from

Millersville State College did their practice training as school-teachers.

We had one large room as our homeroom with close to 100 students. Partitions were pulled through the rooms to make four smaller rooms for classes. Here I was introduced to algebra, civics and art classes. We did some finger painting, which I never heard of before. Civics class was so difficult. I remember bursting into tears when I flunked a Civics test. We studied a Shakespeare play. I could hardly understand the meaning, but my mother came to my rescue and she got some meaning out of "Macbeth" for me. She also knew something about algebra. Mother only had an eighth grade education, but her teacher was Miss Edna Lipp, who gave excellent training to elementary grades students at Harmony Hall. This was the same building in which I attended eighth grade many years later.

We had gym class in ninth grade. I learned to wear a gym suit and take public showers in the girls shower room. I did exercises on the big rings and threw some basketballs. We did some line dancing. I don't think I told Mother about some of these things. She would not have understood at that time. Those were the days I learned to use underarm deodorant, called Mum. Mother explained to me that this cream should be used between the days we took a bath. You rubbed it on with your fingers. I began to have some new girlfriends.

Some of these relationships were maintained throughout our adult lives.

After ninth grade our class went to the Manor Township High School in Millersville. We joined new students who had attended ninth grade in the high school. In my sophomore year I started taking Latin and two years of French the next years. I enjoyed home economics class, grammar and literature. I liked learning about people and cultures. In my senior year we needed to write a paper on the subject of the work we wanted to prepare for after we graduated, and do some research on where to get training for that work. I could not think of any career better than taking care of a large lawn and garden. My research proved that Pennsylvania State College

would have courses to offer for that career. I was not a super student. Being a B or C student satisfied me and I was thankful to receive a diploma in 1941 from Manor Township High School.

The next winter my parents decided I could go to Harrisonburg, VA, to the

Eastern Mennonite College for a six weeks term of Bible study. A few of my girlfriends went too and we had a wonderful time learning to know some new young people, new teachers of the Bible and new spiritual insights. This concluded my formal education.

Ready to graduate from
Manor Township High School, 1941

The four Garber girls—Ruth, Jean, Anna Martha and Marian.

When I was 13 years old we moved to the Herr homestead near New Danville, PA

Ready to go to school; Ruth to ninth grade and Jay to first grade.

Ruth, Anna Martha, Jean, Marian and Jay.

CHAPTER TWELVE

Farm Work As Daddy's Helper

Learning to work comes easily when those around you enjoy what they are doing. It has meaning when it is connected to one's existence.

My parents produced most of our food. They had extra help to do the work there on the farm at Bossler Corner. As a young girl I would ride along with Daddy to Stackstown, near Maytown, to the Baer residence to bring Billy Baer and his sister Flossie to help Mother with gardening and canning the vegetables and fruit in the summertime. Daddy brought Teddy Ney, from Marietta, who stayed for the week, to help with planting and harvesting. There was a series of families living in the tenant house on the hill, and the husband of the family worked on our farm year round. The family I remember most was the Roy and Mary Graybill family who came to us from

Juniata County. We developed a close friendship with the Graybill family and visited them through the years after they moved back to their family farm in Juniata County.

Even though there were always farm hands to help, there was still work for my sisters and me. There was a pile of wood back of the house. Being the oldest child, I was taught to throw those big chunks of wood through the cellar window to burn in the furnace when the weather was cold. It was a back -breaking job. Some of the pieces would be so large that they barely fit into the hole. It was so hard on my young, tender hands.

There were pullets to feed out on the range. It wasn't easy to open the burlap feed bags by pulling the threads just right that were used to sew the bags shut, in order to fill the bucket. My sister, Marian, and I put the buckets on the express wagon and pulled the wagon out to the feeders on the ground around the range shelters. It seemed so difficult to do that procedure. We needed to feed the cows their chop. Chop is ground ear corn that Daddy dumped into the feed chest. My job was to feed the grain to the cows. Daddy had a chart tacked above the chest with each cow's name on it. He had a scale in the feed chest with a big pan on top. I knew each cow's name. The chart said something like "Daisy--1 ½ pounds Larro Dairy feed (we bought that from the mill), 2 pounds corn chop and 2 ½ pounds beet pulp." I learned to add fractions on the feed scales as I fed the 10 or 12 cows. As Daddy emptied the bags of Larro feed he would shake and shake the bags into the chest. We asked him why he shook so long. He usually answered, "I'm shaking the profit out." That was during the depression days. But actually, I think he was of the same mind as his mother who didn't want to lose a grain of rice. Daddy shook the last bit of shredded wheat out of the box at the breakfast table, too.

Daddy raised tobacco in those days. He said he needed something for the tenant farmer to do in the wintertime as well as in the summer. So in the early springtime the tobacco steamer would come in the lane with his steam engine rig. He put large pans on the areas that were prepared as seed beds for tobacco plants. These pans had a hose connected to them. The other end of the hose was connected to the steam engine where the man fired the coal to heat the water that produced the steam. The steam killed the weed seeds. Then Daddy would sow the seed that he saved from a few of the last year's seed heads.

These beds needed to be watered almost daily. Daddy had a nozzle on the water hose and my job was to water those beds. He would mark off a certain distance and have an alarm clock nearby. He would say, "Water this space for 10 minutes." So I stood there sprinkling back and forth over each space the designated amount of time. Some days it was cold and sometimes it was pretty hot standing there in the sun for an 8 to 12 year old girl, who would rather be doing something else.

There was tobacco muslin over the seed beds. After the plants were large enough, Daddy took the muslin off and the plants were soon ready to pull and transplant in the field. He placed a wide board across the beds with supports at each end, so the board would not smash the plants. We would get on this board and on our hunkers we would pull the plants out one by one. Here again the bed needed to be watered enough so the roots did not come off the plant. I watered until I was old enough to get on the board and my younger sister did the watering. Then we would place the plants in a big box and take the boxes to the field where they would be replanted. I was old enough to help plant a couple years before we moved away from that farm. That was hard work. Each plant got a squirt of water as it entered the ground. Two people rode on the planter to do this planting. Grandpa Garber often drove the horses that pulled the planter.

Our cows grazed in the pasture near the barn and house in the summer time. Daddy would call "Come moose" when it was time for them to come into the barn again for feeding and milking. He opened the gate and surely they were ready to come as he called, and would head directly for the door to the cow stable. They knew which stall to walk into and soon their chain was around their neck. I learned to take the chain which was fastened to the wooden trough and fasten the ends together at their necks.

Milking the cows was another daily job. I learned to milk by hand just before Daddy bought an electric Surge milking machine. Sometimes the cow did not like the young hands that milked her. She would come up with that back leg and kick my arm right down. I would be sitting on a one legged wooden stool and it would almost knock me over. I didn't like when she would switch her tail either. Daddy sprayed the backs of the cows with fly spray, so that the cows would not switch so much. I learned to use the Surge milking machine before we moved to New Danville. I could put the milking machines on and take them off. Dad insisted it was done just right, so it would not hurt the cow's udder and she would let her milk down correctly. We placed the strap, called a sursingle, over the cows back, hooked it together under her belly and then hung the pail on it under the cow. We needed to be careful not to allow the vacuum to be disturbed, so the lid would not pull off when we placed the cups on the teats. When we could not feel any more milk coming through the rubber teat cups, then we held the tube tight and the cup would drop off.

Daddy always tried to have the best cows possible. We weighed the buckets of milk and marked it down for each cow twice a day. He would feed them according to how much milk they gave, or rather what he thought their potential was. That is why we weighed the feed so accurately. The Holstein cows were purebreds and Daddy named each new heifer calf with the prefix "Spring Lawn" because our farm had a spring in the lawn. The name of the dam and part of the name of the sire was added to the prefix to identify the calf. We also used the prefix "Spring Lawn" after we moved to New Danville, because that farm had a spring in the lawn as well. A cow's name included the farm name, the sire's name, the dam's name and the "barn" name. For example, "Spring Lawn Lucifer Paclamar Irene."

Daddy tried to raise the best alfalfa hay for the cows. During haymaking time I had some jobs also. I was about nine or ten when Dad taught me to guide the horse up and down the barn hill when the hay was unloaded in the barn. There was a rope fastened to the singletree behind the horse. The rope pulled a large fork that Dad stuck down into a load of loose hay and pulled a lever that made it grab the hay. Then I was to guide the horse down the hill while the rope pulled around a pulley up at the peak of the roof and then across a track to the hay mow. I needed to make the horse go far enough to get the fork load into the mow and then Dad would unlock the lever with a thinner rope and the hay would drop into the mow. One or two men would then spread it around 'til the mow was full. Sometimes the horse would get balky and Dad would say "A little further, Ruth. Go a little further." I would need to pull that jockey stick that was fastened to the bit in the horse's mouth, harder and say some words that would encourage the horse to pull those last couple of feet. Then I would lead the horse back up the hill again.

After the young pullets on the range were starting to lay eggs, they were put in crates at night when they were easy to catch in the dark. Then they were moved to the chicken house. The straw on the chicken house floor was nice and clean and the roosts had been cleaned and the feeders were washed. The nests had new straw in them on which the hens could lay their eggs. There may have been 100 hens housed in that little hen house. Again I was taught to take the chicken mash from the feed chest and fill the feeders with a scoop, not too full or the hens would scratch it out.

Daddy often whistled while he was working. One day I learned to whistle. I was standing by the feed chest, trying to make my lips be tight enough, with a little hole for a whistle to come out. I tried and tried and finally, yes, I made a noise and I could whistle. I often whistled while I washed the milk pails in the milk house. It sounded good in there and I thought the folks could not hear me so well.

There was always garden work to be done in the summer time. I enjoyed working in the lawn or garden with Mother. She and I both liked to trim bushes and pull weeds. I guess it was the end result that made it such fun. It always looked so neat to see the garden freshly hoed and the cement walks looking so tidy.

Our farm was named "Spring Lawn Farm." The walk was important because it led to the spring in the lower lawn. That is where we put our perishable food. It was a rather elaborate place. We went down the walk and over the grass to the entrance. Then we went down about six cement steps and across a flat cement stone, which was over the water, to an area that was solid cement with water on three sides. In the summer time we made many trips to that arched, cool spot. We kept the milk in a container resting in the water for our table use. We had a large, blue and white agate water pitcher in which we carried drinking water from the spring in hot weather. Someone needed to bring a pitcher of water to the house several times a day. One time I went down to get water and behold, there was a green snake across that flat stone! I turned so quickly and ran to the kitchen for Daddy to go quickly to see that snake. He grabbed a garden hoe and carefully descended the steps and managed to kill the snake. He said it was only a harmless garden snake. To me it was a nightmare, happening in broad daylight. I don't like to see snakes to this day.

Farm work included making large meals for the threshermen who came to help at harvest time. Mother was good at making beef that she had canned in the winter time, or ham that was cured in the attic. She mashed potatoes just right with plenty of warm milk and some butter mixed in. There usually were vegetables in the garden or canned green beans. And we usually had cabbage slaw. Sometimes she noticed there was not enough bread on hand, so she quickly stirred up some biscuit dough and in a short time the flakiest product was pulled out of the oven and served piping hot. Mince meat pies were her specialty. In the winter time she had canned the mincemeat filling in two-quart jars. This recipe included ground beef, apples, raisins, oranges, sugar and cider. Boston cream pie was her other specialty for the threshermen's dessert.

At silo filling time these meals were repeated. The neighbor men would gather to help each other at these times. If one would overhear a conversation between the harvest hands, one could perhaps hear these men discussing the food at the various farm kitchens. Some women were known to be extra good at serving big, tasty meals. The weather was usually hot at such times and the children, many times, carried jars or tin buckets of lemonade or meadow tea to the thirsty men.

Daddy went to market at Columbia. Many jobs were connected with this weekly event. I did not like to wash carrots. A large bucket full of carrots was dug from our garden and then we needed to scrub the brown soil off each one in that bucket of water. It took so long to get to the bottom to find the last little carrot.

We dressed chickens for market too. Daddy would catch the chickens that looked like they were not laying eggs any longer. He had a long, thick wire with a hook on the end and he would go after that certain chicken and hook it by the leg, then pull it to himself. He would carry it to the block of wood and chop the head off. We used a large bucket of boiling water to dip the chicken in after it stopped kicking. This was called scalding the chicken. A minute or so later the feathers could be pulled or rubbed off easily. Then it was ready to be singed. Mother would roll up some newspaper and strike a match to it outdoors. As it burned she held the chicken by its legs and let the flames burn off the pin feathers and hair as she turned it all around over the flame. Then the chicken was ready to dress. She would cut open the chicken and pull out the things that were inside. It always fascinated me as she found the egg sack, where perhaps some egg yolks were forming at different sizes. She got the gizzard out and cut it open to pull out the food sack where the corn was being ground up. She found the liver, which had a tiny green sack on it to cut away. It was the gall bladder. Mother was always careful to cut around it so it would not spread any of its bitter juice over the liver. Last of all she found the craw. This was beside the wind pipe and as she pulled it out she was careful it did not tear, because it had freshly eaten corn or mash in it.

Now it was ready to wash out thoroughly and then she tucked the legs into the divided vent. It was neatly finished and ready for market. This was repeated several times, so that Daddy had a nice display of vegetables, dressed chickens, eggs and perhaps some early apples at the market stand.

I often went with Daddy to market. We drove in the Model T Ford truck. If it was raining I watched Daddy use the windshield wiper by hand, turning the handle  back and forth. We had a hard climb on the way home at the hill on which our tenant house was built. Seems we could hardly get up that hill without Daddy changing to low gear. But he would always smile when, sure enough, we made it up and around the corner. At market the folks came to buy their weekly food supply of fresh meats and produce. Usually Daddy would give me a nickel to buy a nice big ice cream cone. I felt so important. I was Daddy's helper. One day there was one chicken left at the end of the day. We stopped on the way home at a large house up on the hill in Marietta. He took the chicken to the door and sold it to the lady for one dollar. That was a relief to have them all sold before going home.

When we moved to the New Danville farm our chores changed. A larger cow stable was installed. Now the cows put their heads through their own stanchion and when each cow was in their place we pulled a lever that tied the whole line of cows at one time. We pushed a cart in front of the mangers and used a scoop to feed them. We had a new milking machine to use. One evening I poured the milk from the pail to the milk bucket which we used to carry the milk to the milk house. One of the cows gave a bucket full. I kept pouring and it ran down one side of the bucket. Daddy reprimanded me loudly for filling it too full. I answered, "Well, it isn't full on the other side, so I just kept pouring." That evening Dad came to my bedroom and said he was sorry he talked to me so sharply. It meant a lot to me to know he did not feel good about his loud words to me. Actually, it seemed difficult for him to acknowledge his impatience with anyone, including my mother and the hired helpers. His temper let loose at times.

I was needed in the fields many times. I was trained to use the side rake to rake the hay into windrows for the hay loader to run it up to the wagon. We used mules for that job. One day Dad borrowed a mule from Grandpa Herr, who lived a quarter mile across the meadow. This mule got very contrary for me and would periodically lie down on the job. Dad, who was loading hay, would need to stop the tractor and get this mule to rise again to finish the job. It happened several times that day. I wonder if the mule felt I was out of place or if he was at the wrong place.

———

When I was about 16 years old Dad taught me to drive the tractors. He bought a caterpillar tractor from Uncle Elvin when we moved to the Herr farm. My mother learned to drive that caterpillar using levers to guide it instead of a steering wheel. We had a fox terrier dog that learned to ride on the fenders of this tractor. After I was old enough to do that job, mother didn't need to drive the tractor so often. When I was about 18 years old Daddy bought a John Deere H tractor and I needed to get acquainted with driving that for raking hay. Dad would always say, "Yes, you can do it. I will show you how!"

We only raised tobacco a few years after we moved to New Danville. There were some new convictions among the Mennonite farmers. If it was wrong to smoke tobacco, then it was also wrong to raise tobacco. So it became popular to convert the tobacco sheds into chicken houses. We now had up to 500 chickens and the egg man would come weekly for the cases of eggs that were weighed into small, medium and large categories. That was work the girls could do in our house cellar. Not raising tobacco gave some extra ground to use for other crops. The farmers were encouraged to raise tomatoes for a contractor. In the summer extra help was needed to pick tomatoes by hand. They were paid about ten cents for each half-bushel basket they picked. This was another back-breaking job for the ladies and boys in the community. But they all liked the extra pocket money. We could pick about 50 to 100 baskets per day, according to our age.

Besides the farm work for us girls, there were jobs in the house. When I was eight years old I had the privilege to go to my Uncle Norman Garber's home near Mount Joy for 4-H club in the summer time. Uncle Norman's daughter Peggy was my favorite cousin. The leader, Miss Forbes, Farm and Home Economist Agent, taught me to hold a needle, put a thimble on my right middle finger and sew a hem in an apron. 4-H only lasted one or two summers for me. I gradually learned to sew with Mother's treadle sewing machine. Mother taught me to cut out a dress from a pattern when I was a teenager. At high school Miss Frantz taught me to make a wool jacket. From there I learned to make most of my dresses. After I had six daughters I made dresses and many skirts for them. I bought a pattern to make a shirt for our son one time, but it seems I never had time to do that.

I learned to cook as I watched my mother. She seldom followed a recipe very closely. So I learned to use what was on hand and make the things we were hungry for. I learned to make pie crusts and bake cakes. We started freezing the garden vegetables around the time I turned 20 years old. The deep freezers were not available until after the Second World War. We first used the lockers at local cold storage plants. We canned many quarts of fruit from local orchards. These were things I knew how to do before I got married. We kept the house clean, but that was never the priority for my mother; our house was usually presentable.

Ready for church with Grandma Herr at Spring Lawn Farm, the Herr homestead near New Danville, PA.

L-R: Ruth, Jay, Grandma (Sue) Herr, Jean, Marian, and Anna Martha.

CHAPTER THIRTEEN

The Great Depression

The Depression days cover the years from 1929 to 1935, when we still lived in the Bossler Corner. Herbert Hoover was President of the United States when the "crash" took place. Many people lost their bank accounts as the banks closed their doors. Other accounts were frozen for a few years. The stock market crashed and "times were hard," as the familiar picture is given.

The years before that time brought prosperity to lots of businesses, including farming. Our family had a new Ford Model A car in 1928 and I remember Daddy trading it in for a 1929 model for $100, thinking that was good business. We were working hard and earning money.

I did not understand the problems that came on the scene. I knew we could not buy much that was new. I didn't know we were poor. We seldom went shopping. Everyone learned to "make do" with what they already had. We had an advantage, living on the farm in those days. We had our garden from which vegetables were canned. The orchard had apples for sauce and apple butter. There was a poor cow to butcher. We canned the tenderloin and made bologna from the tougher parts. Hams were made from the pigs we butchered. We knew some folks in town who hardly had enough food. One time a family drove in our lane and the lady asked if we had a half of ham to spare. I remember Mother taking the meat saw and cutting some slices off for them.

Money was not only scarce, but Mother Nature gave us some hardships in those years. Grasshoppers multiplied one summer and ate the young alfalfa leaves off the stems, so that the whole crop was lost for haymaking. One day the broom handle on the porch was covered with grasshoppers. I was about eight years old. We needed to work hard. Daddy paid $5.00 per week to the hired hand that lived in the tenant house. That family had free rent, the milk they needed, their garden and the eggs they could use for their family of 4 children.

My brother, Jay, was born in 1933. Mother said they never had his picture taken at the studio because they could not afford it. I remember having 25 cents to buy a Christmas present for Daddy. Marian and I were dropped off at the dry goods store in Elizabethtown to see what we could get him for 25 cents. That's the first shopping I remember doing on my own. We found some red handkerchiefs that looked good for a farmer. We may have bought two or three of them with that quarter.

Christmas came. What would we girls get for Christmas? We each had a doll by that time. Yes, mother thought of something for us. She made a new doll blanket for each of our doll babies. It seemed so special to us. We also looked forward to the new paper doll books our mother found for us. We had fun dressing the boys and girls and little babies with their new cut-out wardrobes.

But what could we give mother? Daddy had that planned. He got her a Barlow paring knife for kitchen use. That was a kind of pocket knife, but it was very sharp. We had a fun idea. We wrapped it in a bit of paper and then buried it in a bushel basket among a lot of crumpled newspaper pages. It didn't take much to make everyone happy in those days. Mother used that good, sharp knife for many years.

On butchering day, February 15, 1934, the chimney to our washhouse furnace, which had two iron kettles on it, caught fire and burned the annex to our house. Mother saw the flames coming up from around the chimney when she came from helping to milk at the barn. She quickly told Daddy and he phoned the fire company. Mother handed me one-year-old baby Jay and commanded me to take him and my three sisters to stand at the barn until someone came for us.

I can still see those flames eating their way across the roof of the building that contained the summer kitchen, wash house and a large bedroom upstairs for the hired man. The fire engines arrived about the time a couple uncles and aunts came for us children. The Lancaster newspaper had a headline the next day, reporting "100 firemen and neighbors fight fire to save the house in West Donegal Township."

I remember that the ladies at the Elizabethtown Mennonite Church made dresses for me and my two sisters to replace the school dresses that were in the wash basket that burned in the wash house that night.

That summer there was a great wind storm that blew down our silo, and the tobacco shed in the pasture collapsed. After that storm they built a new, smaller annex to replace the wash house (Mother called it the "laundry" after that) and they built a new tobacco shed along the lane to replace the one that blew down. Grandpa Garber had insurance to cover the damaged buildings and my parents had insurance to cover the contents. When they listed the contents, they forgot to mention Daddy's gun, which was stored on the curve on the stairway. I don't know if they were ever compensated for that loss.

One autumn day Daddy said, "Ruth, I want you to go along to town with me. We are going to try to sell some of these apples from our orchard." So off we went in the model T Ford truck. He parked along the street and gave me 3 apples in my hands. "Go to the door of each house and ask if they would like to buy some apples," he instructed me. I felt very scared and shy as I rang the first doorbell. Upon answering the doorbells the ladies would generally say, "No, I don't need any apples." I think they were 25 cents for a peck. One child answered a door. He called back to his mom, inquiring if she wanted to buy some apples. In no uncertain terms she answered, "No." I did not like this job and Daddy didn't sell many either, so after about an hour we went back home. I have a feeling apples were among the luxuries for town people in those days.

We raised puppies during those years. Our dog, Laddie, was a purebred Airedale dog. Daddy would recognize when she was in heat and brought a male Airedale to our barn where Laddie was tied in the granary. This was mysterious to me. The dogs did not like being tied up in the barn. After a week Daddy would take the male dog back and let Laddie run again. A few months later, sure enough, Laddie would have a litter of pups. We just loved those puppies. Before they were 6 weeks old, we would dress them in doll clothes and pretend all kinds of games with them. Then it was time to sell them. I think he would get one dollar for each puppy. I remember he would place an ad in the newspaper and some folks were rich enough to pay some money for them.

We sold rags in those days. A man would drive his truck in our lane about once a year to buy feed bags. He would ask Mother if she had any rags to sell. Yes, Mother had a rag bag. This was her opportunity to sell them. They were things that had holes too large to mend. The man had a little scale and would hang the bag on the hook and check how many pounds it was. I believe he may have paid her 1 or 2 cents for a pound. After the man left with part of our worn out wardrobe Mother would divide the money she received among us four girls. Each girl got about 4 or 5 cents and we were told to put that in our little chrome barrel banks. Our banks rattled with our money.

At Christmas time Grandpa Herr stacked silver dollars for each of his 10 grandchildren. One by one we picked off our silver dollar from that stack. I was the oldest of the grandchildren and got the top one. It was an impressive ceremony. That money went in our banks too.

One time our neighbor had a public sale before they retired from their farm. Our school was closed that afternoon and all the children were allowed to walk to the sale. It turned out my Grandma Garber's brother, Great Uncle Henry Eby, was at the sale. I said "Hello" to him and talked so grown-up-like with him. He was so kind. He reached in his pocket and gave me 10 cents. Yes, a dime just for me. There was a stand there where they sold penny candy. I felt so rich. I decided to pick out 10 pieces of candy. One kind of candy had a finger ring around it. It was my first ring. I had quite a nice little bag full of candy. I quickly slipped the ring on my finger. It was so special!

For some reason, my parents wanted me to learn to play the piano even though money was scarce. Mother usually took me by automobile about five miles to Elizabethtown every Friday that summer to the piano teacher. The lessons cost 25 cents and we got every fifth lesson free. The piano we had was given to her by her papa when she was a young girl. They only had a pump organ before that and mother begged for a piano like some of her relatives had in Virginia.

The depression years taught us many things. We learned the truth that "A penny saved is a penny earned." "If one does not work, he should not eat." "Better days ahead." And above all, our faith in God was strengthened. His Son, Jesus, said "And, lo, I am with you always, even to the end of the world."

Franklin Delano Roosevelt was elected President in 1934. He seemed to have all sorts of new jobs for the unemployed. There was new hope for our country to get on its feet again. Many new cars were made. Projects for road repair and bridge building were planned. Somehow money began to cir-culate again and people could buy more things. Instead of having just one new dress for Sunday, we had two or three. I started junior high with three new dresses and a new sweater. But we still needed to work hard and save as much money as we could.

CHAPTER FOURTEEN

Friendships Through The Years

As you know, I was the only girl in my first grade class, but the children from all the grades played together on the playground. I liked the boys and since I did not have any brothers to play with, I was interested in what they had to say. Simon Kraybill was my cousin in second grade. His parents brought him to our home early one day. We walked to school together that morning. "I'm going to marry you when I grow up," I declared as I looked at him with admiration. "Oh, Ruth, don't you know you can't marry your cousin?" That was news to me, but I remembered that and kept looking for someone that would be as nice as Simon.

One boy gave me a whole stick of chewing gum one day. I never had a whole stick of gum in my mouth before. We always needed to share a stick with a sister if we did get chewing gum at all. When Chiclets became available, Daddy bought a box of them because they reached around the family better.

Playing with boys didn't happen very often in our family. My brother was 10 years younger than I was. We did have boys living in the tenant house. The first one who came to play with us was Phares Heisey. He was two years older than I was. We played horse and cow at the yard fence. Phares would pull off some long grass and put it inside the picket fence and then we girls would stand outside the fence and pretend to eat the grass. Mother told us that rabbit clover was OK to eat. So then we pulled that tender three leafed clover off and we would actually nibble some of that.

We had two double school desks to play with in our yard. Daddy was a school director in those days. One of the schools wanted to get rid of the double desks and use single desks instead. So Daddy brought two of them to our home. He also got sample school books since he was a Director. We were so pleased to have a Primer and also a first and second grade book among the collection. Phares was the second grader and could read. The younger girls looked at pictures. I was the teacher and we enjoyed playing school. I asked my little sisters to name all the things on the pictures.

We each had a doll and a bed for our dolls. I named the china doll, Kelton Richard, even though it looked like a girl baby.

We had a tea set that my Grandmother Herr played with when she was a child. We made tea by filling the tiny cup three fourth full of water from the tea pot and then filling it with milk from a tiny cream pitcher and then adding a bit of sugar. We had raisins and tiny slices of carrots on our plates. We had a graham cracker for dessert. We usually got very silly at our parties and later needed to sober up when we started to play church. We sang "Jesus Loves Me" and Marian sometimes started to preach. Usually our babies started to cry and we would need to "take them out." That broke up our playtime for that day.

Sometimes I was invited to go to my friend Pearl Garber's home after church on Sundays. There we would have more tea parties and play games such as Dominoes, Old Maids or Uncle Wiggly. There was not much chance to play with boys.

At the New Danville farm a young man, named Bob Wilson, helped me do the milking sometimes. We talked about going to Rocky Springs Park and other interesting activities. As the years went by my girl friends started to talk about their boyfriends. When I was 16 years old, I learned to drive the car and passed the driver's test. I enjoyed talking with Norman, a boy across the aisle in English class. We talked about driving cars and passing the driver's test. He milked cows and so did I. He went to Millersville Mennonite Church and I went to New Danville Mennonite Church.

One evening when I was a 9th grader I was invited to a party for some of the neighboring young fellows and girls. We played games at a long dining room table at the Stehman farm nearby. That was exciting to have boys and girls playing together. I remember being waitress at Pearl Garber's wedding in the Bossler's Church area when I was about 17. I needed to wait 'til I was 18 to start going out with the young fellows. Finally it happened. I was a senior in high school. There were other Mennonite boys in my class. There was Glenn, Amos and Christ. Our class went to Washington DC for two days when we graduated. The Mennonites went sightseeing in a taxi while the other classmates went to a movie. We had fun being together as a last fling for our school days.

A Girl Party at the Garber home, 1941. We invited school friends, church friends, cousins and siblings.

The upper teenage girls had lots of fun in those days. Many times the mailman would bring a post card inviting me to a friend's home on a Sunday afternoon for a "Girl Party." About 20 to 50 young girls would gather at a home to play group games and have refreshments out on the lawn. Some of the girls had boyfriends who would come to take them home in the evening.

When I was in high school I was invited to join the Sew-So Club. This was a group of Manor Twp High School Mennonite girls. There were a dozen of us that met a few hours on one Saturday each month. We took our crocheting and embroidery work along and we worked at that while we laughed and talked about our boyfriends and activities. Helen Mann Herr is the only one of this group that is living today besides

The Sew-So Club met at my home Circa 1942

myself. This group, along with our young families, had an annual reunion for many years.

When I was 18 years old I had a girl party in our lawn. The picture shows 40 girls besides my siblings were guests. Some of my young girl cousins were among the guests. We played some fun games and had ice cream and cake. Actually that was my last project for Home Economics class that year.

A few times I was invited to the Brubaker "Shi Maid Shack," a cabin in the Brubaker's meadow near the Chickies Creek. There was a group of girl friends who spent the night at the cabin. Our boyfriends came for supper the next evening and took us home. We shared a close friendship for many years along with our families. Today Reba Witmer Miller and I both live at Landis Homes.

My Shi Maid group of girlfriends. We prepared supper for our boyfriends who came to take us home. L-R: Anna Shertzer, Norma Rohrer, Lillian Wenger, Thelma Longenecker, Ruth Garber (me), Mary Stauffer, Martha Rutt, Helen Brubaker, Reba Witmer.

CHAPTER FIFTEEN

Courtship And Marriage

The custom was for the guys to drive their new car to a girl's home, blow the horn and ask someone for a certain girl to come out to talk with them. This happened a number of times for me. I would go out to the car and then the guy would ask for a date. There were dates to go to Sunday evening church services and invitations to my girlfriends' homes after church where we would play games and have a treat. Then the fellow would take me home and we would visit a short while. By 12 o'clock he generally asked for another date and then went home. I had dates with quite a few guys but none of them suited me well enough to think we should continue dating; and there were times the guy did not ask for another date.

My daddy had opinions about who I should date. One day when we drove to Lancaster together, he pulled into a parking space on East Orange Street, and turned to me. I could tell it was something important. He said, "Ruth, I don't want you to go with (the young man who recently asked me for a date). His father doesn't treat his mother right." Another time he advised me to cut off a relationship because the young man's family didn't treat the grandmother right. She was mentally ill, and they kept her in a room upstairs, and didn't let her come down to be with the family. When the time came, Daddy approved of Elmer Rohrer. I now know this was the Lord leading me to the right person.

In 1941 World War II began and gradually, by 1942, there were shortages of sugar, butter, shoes, gasoline, furniture and appliances. Rationing stamps were issued by the government for many items. People needed to go to a designated place to receive these stamps. I helped to give out sugar stamps at the Harmony Hall School in 1943. One needed to report how much sugar you had in the house. Then stamps were given for a few pounds per week, according to the number in the household. We saved our stamps in order to have some sugar for canning fruit in the summer time.

Sunday, March 8, 1942 there was a knock on our front door at the New Danville farm house. When I opened the door, it was someone I did not know. However, I knew his brother and I could tell they were related. He said he was Elmer Rohrer. "Would you be available for a date this evening?" I was so impressed that he did not just blow the horn and ask for me to come out to his car. He was polite and manly enough to come to my door.

Well, I had plans to be in charge of children's meeting at the Vine Street Mennonite Church in Lancaster that evening. I was going to take my sister, Anna Martha, along and our cousin, who was her age, plus my friend, Edith Herr. The young girls decided not to go if I had a date, but Elmer consented to take Edith along with us. We dropped Edith off at her home after church and Elmer and I visited at my home that evening. As we look back, we both enjoyed the times we shared from one week to another.

I had dates with some fellows my age that had later models of cars. The gear shifts were now on the steering columns. Elmer's car had the older style. The gear shift was on the floor. Our young hired helper made the comment to me one day, "Ruth, I see it's not the kind of car your boyfriend has that suits you." "No, I go by the kind of guy that drives the car," I emphatically answered.

Again, the custom was to have only one or two dates per week with any young man. This became a necessity as gas became very scarce. We needed to stay close to home for our dates. Some men were drafted into the service in those years.

Elmer's dad bought a farm in 1942, so that Elmer and his brother could be deferred because of the farm work. Much food was needed for the servicemen. The young men were being drafted and farm helpers were scarce. Elmer was almost three years older than I was so lots of his friends had been drafted. Some conscientious objectors chose Civilian Public Service, offered by the government, which was work other than fighting in the military. Building parks and roads, working in mental hospitals, forestry and fire fighting in the National Forests were some of the options for conscientious objectors.

Elmer and I felt God leading us together. He was called as Sunday school teacher for a class of young boys at Millersville Church. We would study the Sunday school lesson together on Saturday evenings. We had some double dates with other young couples, and many times we would get on spiritual subjects as we visited together. There were evangelistic meetings to attend. There were ministers who greatly challenged us to remain pure in our courtship days and to find ways to serve the Lord in our daily living. Some challenged the farmers to stop raising tobacco. That was a major decision for many young men to consider.

The summer of 1943 our courtship became more serious. Several evenings Elmer rode the eight miles from his home to mine on his bicycle, since his gas supply was so low. We took walks on Sunday afternoons and stayed at his home or my home for supper. I began to appreciate Elmer's Christian character, his honesty, his integrity and the manly decisions he made when under stress. He had a great sense of humor, which I enjoyed. I began to feel my love grow deeply for him. I felt he admired my principles and my actions when in a group and my spiritual insights. I felt he might propose to me someday.

Mother and I were shopping for dress material at Watt and Shand's, a department store in Lancaster, one summer day. I needed to make a new dress to be a gift receiver at a friend's wedding. After we decided on a few yards for that dress, I spied a display of fabric that really caught my eye. There it was. This was war time and fabrics were scarce, especially white fabric for wedding dresses. There was white dotted Swiss marquisette hanging on display for $1.00 per yard. Only certain nice fabrics cost that much in those days.

"Mother, do you think we ought to buy enough of that pretty white fabric for my wedding dress?" I approached this idea with caution because, no, I was not engaged to Elmer as yet. But the war was still going strong and there was the possibility that I could not find such pretty material later on. Dear Mother -- she agreed with me that we should buy four yards so that we would have it on hand "if and when I needed it."

Having done that, Mother and I agreed we would tell no one but Daddy.

One evening my 10 year old brother asked me, "Ruth, which boyfriend do you really like the best?" I did not hesitate to tell Jay, "I like Elmer the best!" "So do I," said Jay. "I think Elmer is the best of all!"

MARRIAGE

So then it happened. One August evening my sweetheart asked me to marry him. Oh, yes, I wanted to marry him. We had been in the habit of praying together before Elmer left for home and this night it was so wonderful to ask God to bless this decision for His glory. "I am going to be a wife." Oh, that sounded so fulfilling. I stopped in Mother and Daddy's bedroom before I went to my room that night. "Elmer asked me to marry him," I excitedly reported to them. They shared my delight. Yes, Elmer's dad had a farm near Millersville on Charlestown Road and Elmer wanted me to move into that house with him in the spring.

A while later the date for the wedding was set for February 19, 1944. I would be 21 in January and Elmer would turn 24 in March. We were a mature couple with plans to move to a 97 acre farm, about 10 miles from my parents.

"I am engaged!" The custom was to keep that a secret until almost time for the wedding invitations to go out. But the very thought made me so happy. Our engagement was announced in the mail to relatives and close friends that winter.

We made plans together, but my parents had some suggestions, too, such as, "You will need a kitchen cabinet." "You should have twin beds, because you can rest better that way." I had $100 saved in my dresser drawer from working at the market for $4.00 a day, selling meats and cheese. I had never been reimbursed for work I did on the farm. My parents said they would give me money to furnish the house. Grandma Garber came one day to help make my wedding dress. She said, "Every bride should break a needle on her wedding dress." I guess that was an old superstition. We planned a simple wedding to take place in my home. Church weddings were not allowed at New Danville Mennonite Church in those days. The rules changed when my sister, Marian, got married to Henry Leaman about 3 years later, so their wedding was in the church.

My mother made the guest list. About 100 friends and relatives were invited. I asked my sister, Marian, to be my bridesmaid. Elmer asked his brother, Paul, to be his best man. We had girl friends for waitresses and gift receivers. My parents engaged the Hostetter Catering Services from Mount Joy to make the hot meal. Due to the gas shortage, we needed to stay close to home for our wedding trip. Elmer made plans for us to spend our first night at Hershey Hotel. However, he kept me guessing where we were going `til our wedding day.

We had a beautiful, sunny and warm wedding day. Elmer reminds me sometimes that he got up early that morning to clean out the horse stable, before he dressed for the big occasion. We had a men's quartet to sing several songs after the guests were all seated in the house. "O, Perfect Love" was sung as my sister Marian and I came down the front steps and into the living room, where my beloved Elmer and his brother, Paul, were waiting for us. Our Bishop, Stoner Krady, gave a short message about marriage and then led us in our promises. He asked the questions and we answered "Yes." He then led in a prayer for us. I still remember the kiss that sealed our promises. I was a happy bride. I married the man of my choice and dreams. I felt God's blessing on us. "O, Father Lead Us" was sung as the service was ended. "Thank you, Lord. We trust you. Amen."

Friends served as waitresses at each other's weddings.

Paul Herr-Usher, Paul Rohrer-Best Man, Elmer Rohrer-Groom,
Ruth Garber-Bride, Marian Garber-Maid of Honor, Simon Kraybill-Usher.

Part Three

Our Journey Together

At the kitchen
door of our new
home.

Newlyweds share
dish duty in the
newly updated
kitchen. We didn't
need a kitchen
cabinet because
we had cupboards
installed.

CHAPTER SIXTEEN

"Happily Ever After"
The Onward Journey

I was ready for the adventures of marriage. At least I thought I was. All that night I rehearsed the events of my wedding day. We had left home in our "going away clothes" that Saturday evening. Tin cans rattled as we started out the lane as husband and wife. We stopped about five miles from home for Elmer to remove the cans. There he suggested that we pray to God in thanksgiving for the wonderful mystery of marriage and the day that was now history and that we would never forget. We were on our way, driving 25 miles to Hershey, PA.

As we got off the elevator onto the 3rd floor of the prestigious Hershey Hotel, and walked down the hall, two young ladies came walking toward us. They noticed me with my corsage on my winter coat, arm in arm with my sweetheart. They immediately sang, "Here comes the Bride. Please step aside!" Perfect timing. I was that bride!!

Purity! What a gift! The thrill of being with my lover on our wedding night was worth all the discipline it took during those courtship days. God's plan was fulfilled. Morning came and it was not a dream. This was real. We were going to breakfast as husband and wife. The dining room was lovely. We ordered a half grapefruit and grape nuts cereal, and we had hot chocolate too. I guess it was Hershey's.

We had made plans to go to the Brethren in Christ church in Palmyra that Sunday morning where our friends, John and Ruth Schock, attended. We had dinner and visited with them in the afternoon. In the evening we went to Annville where we had been invited to stay with Marlin and Mabel Weaver, who had been married almost two years earlier. Mabel is Elmer's cousin. They played a good trick on us that night. We finally got to bed in their guest room. We were all nestled down for a good night's sleep. Suddenly a terrific noise started up, coming from under our bed. I grabbed Elmer and we shouted in astonishment. Oh, dear, the vacuum cleaner was under there and the motor was running. It wasn't long 'til we heard laughing out in the hall. Mabel and Marlin had the plug to that machine out in the hall and were waiting for just the right moment to plug it in. It worked. It scared us and gave us a memory that lasted to this day.

We learned later about another episode on our wedding day. As the crew from Hostetter's Catering prepared the wedding meal in our kitchen, an electrical circuit was overloaded, and the power to part of the kitchen cut off. The crew was instructed to keep the oven door closed to conserve the heat. They used a portable stove to finish the meal, and successfully served a delicious dinner for 100 people without Elmer or me knowing there was a problem.

There was not much left of that half tank of gasoline reserved for the wedding trip when we returned to Millersville that Wednesday evening. The days ahead of us were filled with preparations for housekeeping. But one other formality took place two weeks after the wedding day. There was a reception for another group of 100 of Elmer's relatives and friends at the Hostetter Banquet Hall in Mount Joy.

We waited until April first to move to our home in the farmhouse on Charlestown Road. The former owners, Omer and Marie Charles, had public sale and moved to another home nearby. We could now move in and we would start a new adventure in housekeeping as husband and wife. Our new dining room suite, bed room furniture and three piece living room suite were delivered. We had bought an extension kitchen table and six chairs at the Charles' public sale. The kitchen cabinet Mother thought I needed was put into a back room. Elmer's parents had decided some cupboards and a sink should be built in our large kitchen. So the kitchen cabinet was not needed. A neighboring couple decided they needed it in their kitchen, so we sold it to them for $45, which was $5 less than we paid for it. The 4-piece, 18th century-style dining room suite, plus 6 padded chairs cost $210. We were happy to find a three-piece upholstered living room suite with springs. Due to the war, they were not putting springs in the new ones. It was brown brocaded velvet and cost $150. Years later our oldest grandchildren were using the twin beds that were part of our early furnishings.

A new washing machine was not to be found, but we were blessed to find a used Maytag wringer washer for $100. We got a galvanized rinsing tub somewhere for $8.00. It was the hardest challenge to get a kitchen stove. We finally decided on a combination coal and gas stove. We needed the coal part to heat the kitchen and the gas part for cooking in summer time. There were restrictions due to the war on using bottled gas, so we had the stove delivered, but we had to leave it in the crate `til we were able to get the papers properly signed to start using it. So in the meantime we had three round portable oil heaters standing in the kitchen. I used these to cook potatoes and other foods for our meals. I used the spring outside the cellar for our refrigerator.

This farm house was built many years ago. The west end was built in 1804 with beautiful gray native limestone. The east end was built in 1833. There was a wide doorway between the two sections and a large fireplace in the oldest part that was enclosed in more recent years with cupboard shelves built inside. The thick stone walls created deep, wide window sills in every room, perfect for plants or books or stacks of school papers later on. There were fireplaces in two downstairs rooms and two in the upstairs rooms, plus the large one in the cellar. All of these were closed in except the one in the cellar where the large copper kettle hung when it was used for heating water. Here is where we also burned the paper trash as long as we lived in that house.

So, the kitchen where we started housekeeping was a blend of the old style, and some newer features. We had cabinets and a double stainless steel sink on the south side, and the cook stove on the east side. We had cold running water at the sink, and in the east corner was an iron trough with one cold water faucet. Later, we added the refrigerator and a telephone table at the window between the sink and the refrigerator. The "back stairway" went up from the kitchen on the north side, and we put a cot along that wall. Elmer's roll-top desk sat on the west wall.

Elmer went to the barn early in the morning. He would light one or two of those heaters, according to how cold the kitchen was, before leaving the house, in order to warm up the kitchen those chilly April mornings. Then I would dress for the barn and help milk the cows after he had fed them. On Easter Sunday morning I came down the steps and opened the stair door, only to discover the one stove had started to smoke and the kitchen was full of black smoke. I quickly turned off the burner and opened the outside door. What a mess that gave. The woodwork, curtains and windows had a coat of black smoke to clean off. It had a bad odor and it took a while `til we had that all removed. One does what one has to do. This was an example from my early housekeeping days; there are unexpected curves that take extra work and acceptance.

Elmer worked our garden soil, using the horse and plow. He then made rows for planting peas and other early vegetables. I enjoyed the gardening, the yard work, the milking and taking care of the baby chicks. The housework was a different story. I needed to discipline myself to keep the dishes washed, the floors swept and the dusting done regularly. There were no sisters or my mother to do it while I was outside. I needed to prepare three meals a day and plan ahead for laundry and shopping. I knew how these things needed to be done, but I felt pressured to find the time. It was a new challenge for me and I worked hard at it. I liked to see a presentable house but I was not an immaculate perfectionist.

By the middle of the summer we could use our stove. Elmer's mother had given us some baked goodies during the time we had no oven to use. As autumn arrived I decided to give a pumpkin pie to her in appreciation for the way she blessed us. I made it like my mother made them. Mother called the pies "Pumpkin Custard." Elmer liked it but I realized it was not quite the thing he called "Pumpkin Pie." A day or so after I gave the pie to Elmer's dad to take home, we talked together on the phone. Mother Rohrer said, "Thanks for the pie. What kind of pie was that?" "It was a pumpkin pie," I answered. "Oh, Paul thought there was a little pumpkin in it," she replied. Paul was Elmer's brother. You see, his mother used lots more pumpkin in her pies. I asked her what spices she used and she said, "cloves," as if I should know that much.

Now I had a challenge. I tried making a pumpkin pie like his mother made. I used more pumpkin and less milk and I put cloves in the mix and just a little cinnamon sprinkled on the top the next time I made pumpkin pies. Elmer ate his piece and said, "This tastes like my mother's pumpkin pies." Now I knew how to make pumpkin pies. Oh, yes, our cultural differences were showing up.

We lived in a large, limestone farmhouse with a total of 16 rooms, including the four rooms in the brick annex on the back of the house. Throughout the 29 years we lived in that house, another family almost always lived in part of it, or "on the other side of the house," as we said. Helen and Kenneth (Kack) Charles lived there when we moved into the farm house. Helen Charles and I became good friends and shared recipes and ideas. She and Kack were expecting their second child and yes, now we were expecting our first baby in March. These children were born a couple of months apart and both were girls. Ours was Norma Jean, born March 11, 1945. She and June and Louise Charles were the best of playmates in the big lawn, on their tricycles and inside, on the stair steps, playing with dolls and other toys.

Seven children in eleven years

Thinking of Norma Jean's birth, I remember staying in bed at the General Hospital for nine days. I was allowed to dangle my legs and sit on the rocking chair the tenth day after she was born. On the 11th day I could walk the halls, and I went home on the 12th day. These rules are entirely changed today, when most mothers go home just hours after giving birth, or the next day. Those days of "rest" left me weak, so I had a good helper at home for a week or more after our babies were born.

When Norma Jean was a year old, the war was over. We decided it was time for us to take a belated wedding trip to Florida. My parents kept the baby and off we drove for two weeks in the south. That was March, 1946, and there were no interstate highways. New tires were almost unavailable. Elmer had bought four new retreads for on our car and we packed the 1938 Dodge with two extra tires, food, a little canned-heat stove and our suitcases. That was a wonderful trip, except every so often we had a flat tire. Elmer would either patch it or put on another retread. We had hoped to go all the way to Key West but we needed to use the last retread when we got half way between

Changing yet another flat tire during our trip to Florida two years after our wedding.

Homestead and Key West. "We better turn around," Elmer wisely announced. We were able to buy a new tire from a man in Homestead. Actually, that tire got us all the way home. We had seen the palm trees, smelled the orange blossoms, saw the oranges on the trees, picked some grapefruit, visited Ringling Bros. Circus winter quarters and slept in tourist cabins. We had a vacation and called it our honeymoon. It was wonderful.

We were so excited to see our little one-year-old again. Norma Jean had her first birthday while we were gone, and her three aunts and uncle loved the opportunity of having their little niece in their home. But now we were a family again.

When Norma Jean was 2½ years old, our second baby girl was born on September 16, 1947. We named her Susan Ruth after her Great Grandma Herr, whose birthday was also in September. By the time she was born we had a bathroom on the first floor, next to the kitchen. Before this we only had an outhouse in the back yard. We took our baths in the kitchen, in front of the warm oven in the galvanized laundry tub, heating the water on our coal stove or on the gas burners. This new stove also provided hot water to use in our new Maytag washer in the laundry on the first floor. Up until this time, we had heated water in the big iron kettle at the open fireplace in the cellar for the old Maytag washer down there.

In this new bathroom we now had a bucket-a-day stove to heat our bathroom and the water for our new laundry tubs, the sink and bathtub. This stove used about a bucket of coal per day, hence its name. Of course, it also gave about a bucket of ashes every day or so and they needed to be shoveled out carefully, so they didn't make so much dust when dropped into the bucket.

Elmer usually brought in the coal from the arch cellar outside. There was a hole in the top of the arch where the coal was poured down from the truck. We used a space heater in the dining room in the winter time when we needed more than just the kitchen and bathroom heated. There were stove pipes for the smoke, which went through the ceiling to the upstairs and into the chimneys up there. These helped to heat those bedrooms a few degrees warmer as well.

Our son, Jay Elmer, was born February 7, 1949, about 16 months after Sue was born. He was a delightful surprise. Elmer would spend, what seemed to me, a long time standing at the nursery window, looking at his baby boy. God blessed us with our hearts' desire. This child caused me to be very busy. When Jay was a baby, Susie was a busy toddler. She and the neighbor's son, Jimmy Charles, who was about her age, were busy youngsters, often slipping away to unusual adventures, such as crawling under the yard fence toward the road .

Jay had an umbilical hernia from birth. He needed surgery when he was about six months old to repair it. He has only a scar instead of a belly button. He jokingly told his inquiring friends, "I was not born like other people. I was hatched."

Two years later, on March 14, 1951, our Nancy Elaine was born. Her arrival was different from the other three. Having some bleeding before the birthing pains began, I required a sudden trip in the ambulance to the hospital for an emergency cesarean section delivery. Three little heads peered out the dining room window as Elmer's sister Kathryn helped them watch me go out on the stretcher. Nancy's was a placenta-previa birth. As I understand it, that means the placenta was implanted low in the womb and obstructed the birth canal. The condition carries a risk of suffocating the baby in the birth canal during a natural birth, and hemorrhaging for the mother. We rejoiced when both the baby and I were alive by the end of the operation. This was not the end of the surprise, however. There was a cyst on the end of the baby's spine that needed special attention. The doctors said she may need to go to Philadelphia for special surgery to have it removed. My daddy came to the hospital to take pictures of Nancy in case she wouldn't live through this serious surgery.

This report made me quite concerned. I had a head cold and cough. I had an IV tube in my hand and an incision that hurt when I coughed or moved. I cried after Elmer went home that evening and that made my nose all stopped up. I thought I was in the worst of discomfort. It occurred to me that Jesus must have felt something like I did when he hung on the cross. When I came to my senses I realized that certainly he felt far worse than I did. About that time a dear nurse came to my bedside and spoke to me. "Mrs. Rohrer, I believe you know the Lord, don't you?" "Yes," I answered her. "Well, how about we turn this all over to Him? I'm going to give you a shot that will help you rest." It wasn't long 'til I was sleeping.

Morning came and good news followed. The nurse reported that the x-rays showed the cyst on the baby's spine did not open into the fluid in the spine. They would do the operation in the Lancaster hospital, and it would not be as serious as they first thought it was. Nancy developed well and was soon another playmate for her siblings.

About 17 months later another baby girl joined our family. This was Linda Mae, born August 5, 1952. The weather had been extra warm in July that summer. Our doctor said, "The nights will cool down by the end of July." Of course there was no air conditioning and caring for the family was an extra load in such hot weather. Surely enough, the weather got cooler and our little baby had a warm and comfortable welcome. The problem that showed up this time was diarrhea. We did not have disposable diapers in those days and when she was about six weeks old, Linda had as many as 15 dirty diapers a day. Her bottom would get very red and sore if she was not changed promptly each time she made the diaper dirty. It took the doctor many weeks to discover the source of her problem. She was in the hospital for about a week and it cleared up. We brought her home and the problem started up again. I finally decided to try some canned Pet milk for formula. Behold, that cleared up the diarrhea. I told the doctor and he said that's what they were using in the hospital. Oh dear, why didn't they tell me? We came to the conclusion that the new silage fed to the cows in September caused a reaction in Linda's digestive system when she drank cows' milk. It was so wonderful to have a contented three month old baby with a sweet smile.

Baby Esther Louise was born September 25, 1954. Yes, another girl, with deep dimples in her cheeks. Her big sister, Norma Jean, was now 9 ½ years old. She literally took over the baby care. She carried Esther on her hip and entertained her as soon as she came home from school each evening. Esther loved attention and was a happy baby. When she was almost 2 years old she had a bad case of poison ivy on her face. She was admitted to the hospital for special care. When I visited her one afternoon the nurses were having fun pushing her through the halls on a surgical cart.

Once more I went to the doctor, informing him I was pregnant. His nurse said to me, "Well, Mrs. Rohrer, at least I know when you are expecting a baby it will have a warm welcome!" Yes, perhaps this will be a brother for Jay. The children knew we were expecting a baby in the family. Jay was about 7 years old and in second grade. He declared one day, "If we have another girl, I am going to run away." We knew we would make news for the community either way.

The day came. April 9, 1956, our 6th baby girl arrived. Dr. Musselman was there when she appeared. He said, "Well, Ruth, I guess Jay will need to pack his suitcase. It's a girl." I was thrilled to have another girl, born so close to my mother's birthday. Elmer's eyes met mine as I was wheeled to my hospital room. "How about that?!! Another girl!" we marveled. We named this precious one Vera Ann. She was born three days before my mother's birthday.

After five days we took her home and as I held her on the couch, Jay sat beside me and said, "Is this our baby?" "Yes this is our baby girl." "Well, where's my brother?" Jay asked as he sadly looked her over. "Jay, isn't this a sweet baby? Would you like to trade her for another baby?" He pondered the idea a bit and looked me in the eye. "No, I want to keep this one," he said. A few days later we were eating our supper when the baby started to whimper a bit in her small bed in the next room. Jay got off his chair and disappeared into the next room. Moments later he announced, "I got her out!" There he was, carrying this wee bundle out to the kitchen. Only seven years old, but he loved this tiny sister very much.

Sometimes it was like a circus

Busy days followed. God had blessed me with a very good friend in my neighborhood, before I got married. Edith B. Herr was the girl who went with us on our first date. She was in my Sunday school class at New Danville. We kept in touch after Elmer and I started housekeeping. She worked in a home in Lancaster and had a day off each week. She enjoyed coming out to our farm on that day. She liked to help me with gardening and preserving food. As our family grew she helped me 2½ days per week. Her help was appreciated all the more with washing, ironing and gathering eggs. She loved our children and could take care of them when Elmer and I took a day off from farm work once in awhile.

Edith moved to Iowa to help another good friend about the time Esther was one year old. That winter the family got sick with the flu. I remember Nancy sitting on the couch with droopy eyes. Each one needed Mother. I had a big pile of laundry that needed to be hung on the clothesline, but it was a wet day. I heard my neighbor about two miles up the road had a new automatic clothes dryer. I decided to ask if she could dry a load of laundry for me. It would cost me 10 cents per load. "Sure, bring it up," Miriam Charles answered. As I drove up the road I felt so burdened with cares. Suddenly, I remember, God impressed me with the thought that I should lift up my eyes to the horizon and stretch my thoughts beyond the family. As we visited while those clothes were drying, my cares and burdens were lifted. Miriam was a wonderful encourager. It was so good to unburden my heart. I went home with a basket full of dry clothes and a lighter heart, ready to care for the sick family again.

By the time Vera was a baby the automatic washers and dryers were proving themselves. One by one the busy mothers were convinced that using the hot water for just one load of laundry was a luxury we could afford, and clothes did not always need to have fresh air to fluff them up and make them smell good. We decided to purchase an automatic washer and dryer, which were installed in the kitchen. Nylon fabrics were on the market which decreased the ironing load considerably. How did I manage before these conveniences became popular? Having a washer and a dryer and using nylon was indeed almost as good as having a lady come in to help me with the housework.

Another improvement we appreciated in the mid 1950's was the stoker furnace for central heating which replaced the bucket-a-day stove. Elmer drove to Pine Grove, PA, in the coal mining region to bring our coal for the stoker in his blue GMC truck. He parked the truck at the western gable end of the house to run the coal directly to a bin in the cellar near the stoker. Here again the ashes needed to be carried away periodically.

Our children were growing up and going to school. The winter when Vera was a baby, our kitchen looked something like a circus after supper. Elmer needed to go to the barn to bed the cows and give them a rack full of hay from the mow for their evening feeding. Vera Ann would be lying on the couch with her bottle full of milk. Esther would be playing with her dolly or pulling a toy around the kitchen table. Linda and Nancy would be riding their tricycles around the table in this big farm kitchen. Nancy was in kindergarten and she would suddenly ask, "Mommy, may I take my baby sister to school for Show and Tell tomorrow? Please, may I?" "Who would change her diaper, Honey," I inquired. "Oh, Mrs. McCall would. She knows how."

Susie washes dishes, Norma Jean helps Vera Ann with her bottle.

At the same time, Jay was in second grade. He would sit beside the sink where I was washing dishes, reading his 2nd grade lesson to me. I needed to keep reminding him to keep on reading. Susie was in 4th grade. She would be asking me to give out her spelling words one by one. And Norma Jean was in 6th grade trying to read and understand her history lesson in the other room. Did you ever wonder why my hair turned gray at an early age? They say it is all inherited. I wonder.

By 8 o'clock it was bedtime and another scenario took place. I was glad our bathtub was next to the kitchen. Evening baths and bedtime stories did not happen without some good planning and it was no secret that those routines happened when I was very tired. Reading bedtime stories usually happened in the girls' bedroom. Bible stories from Eigermier's big book were important, as the children took turns choosing a story. I would tuck them in their beds with much thanksgiving that my bedtime was close at hand as well. I especially appreciated when Elmer could bring his helping hand on the scene. He could usually make the little ones laugh and settle down without as many warnings as I needed to make. Their prayers were said and then as we left the rooms we would all say "Good night, sleep tight, wake up bright in the morning light, to do what's right with all your might. And so, good night."

Usually that was the end of it, but sometimes we would hear "I'm thirsty." "I'm too hot." "I'm too cold." Or once in awhile one would say "I'm scared," or "My stomach hurts." A loving act or soothing word would follow and soon I was kneeling by my bed saying, "Lord, please help me be a good mother. I really don't know how to handle some of these scenarios and problems." Oh, how I needed to trust my faithful heavenly Father for wisdom.

Yes, I was a happy mother of seven children. I had a great husband. He was a good daddy. We did the best we could. It was a constant challenge. We needed each other. There were hard places and we made mistakes along the way, but God promised us, "Lo, I am with you always, even to the end of the world." I learned to trust Him!

Susan "Susie" Ruth, born 1947, Norma Jean, born 1945,
and Jay Elmer, born 1949

Susie and
Norma Jean
call home
from Grand-
ma Garber's
house

Now we're a
family of six.

Baby Vera
Ann makes it
six girls and
one boy.

Esther Louise, born 1954, Nancy Elaine, born 1951, holding
Vera Ann, born 1956 and Linda Mae, born 1952.

CHAPTER SEVENTEEN

"I" Becomes "We"

In early April, 1944 Ruth and I moved into that gray lime-stone house with white shutters on that Manor Township farm. We were newlyweds, and "I" had become "we." "Lead on dear Father." Yes, we were eager to start this journey to-gether. Ruth had dairy farm experience. Yes, she could milk a cow. In fact she helped milk all twelve of them by hand that first morning. By evening, we had the use of a new Surge milking machine. How nice! The pay scale was simple. We would receive 20 percent of the farm profit and any money made on the chickens was ours to keep. We were in business.

By the next March, 1945 we had a new chapter in our lives becoming evident. I can see Ruth coming from the mailbox toward the house, heavy with child. "My wife, our child," I mused. In her part of this book, Ruth wrote a good coverage on our family life, giving an overview of our seven children and many events that we shared together as a family. I will attempt to fill in some of the blanks.

One event comes to my mind. We had contracted to grow a few acres of baby lima beans. It was harvest time and we were hauling the beans to the vinery near New Danville. As I was driving the tractor and wagon down the hill toward the Slackwater Bridge, the wagon tongue disconnected from the wagon end and fell to the ground. I had to stop that wagon somehow! I jammed the brakes and let the wagon bump the tractor tires a few times to slow the wagon. But then it happened – this time the wagon climbed the tractor tire and pushed the seat front. I moved aside almost enough to escape, but the seat caught me by the seat of my pants, and pinned me to the center hub of the steering wheel. My thanks went to a passing Gunzenhouser Bakery delivery truck driver who came to my rescue. You may note that this is the second story about a person being caught by the seat of his pants, but this one is true. Thank you Lord!

I still have the record books from our early years of farming. Our 1945 year-end summary: $7382.35 less $1476.47 (my 20%) gives a net farm profit of $5905.88.   Chicken profits that year totaled $593.84. The 20% share arrangement remained in place until 1951, when my parents bought a farm for Paul and then my share was raised to 25% of the income.

Paul had married Edith Good on December 20, 1945.

The broiler chicken market was gaining in popularity in 1953, and with Dad's consent we built a six-thousand capacity broiler house on the farm. My carpenter experience was used, with a minimum of outside help to build the chicken house.

In 1956 we bought the farm from Dad. This, in turn helped my parents buy a farm for my youngest brother, Robert, who had married Lorraine Sauder on October 3, 1953. Our purchase price was determined by taking first cost plus improvements and the equipment at a very fair price. The escalated land prices were not a factor.

While Dad and I were not always on the same page in our thinking, we did find a workable solution. We were in the dairy, steer feeding and poultry business. We changed the tobacco shed into a three story laying hen house, and enlarged it to more than double in size. I was the head carpenter. Operating the farm was possible with the help of one full time man, plus some part time help from the children that was always appreciated.

In 1957 a sudden change came into the family. My mother suffered a severe stroke. Mother was in the hospital for six months. This was followed by the services of a Licensed Practical Nurse, Mrs. Shining, who lived in their home. For more than a decade other people came to live with my parents and cared for my mother. There were times when we could communicate with her, but her verbal skills were very limited and she rarely left her bed. Mother spent her last days in Village Vista Nursing Home. She passed into Glory on May 20, 1971 at age 83 years. Two months before Mother died, Dad passed on to Glory on March 19, 1971. He was age 84, and died from a severe stroke. It was during those last fourteen years that Dad proved his love for Mother by his daily visits and with many expressions of tender care. At that time, my family, being bonded in love, reached a peaceable settling of the Elmer B Rohrer estate. Twenty years later, in 1991, the same could be said of the J Clarence Garber family. We are thankful these amiable relationships have been enjoyed by our families to this day.

By 1958, we were a busy, but happy family with seven children. Our 1949 Chevy automobile was getting filled up, and we replaced it with a `57 Chevy station wagon with seats for nine.

The farm in Lebanon County

In 1960, much to our surprise, a realtor from Armstrong World Industries approached us and stated their desire to buy our farm along with five or six other farms in the neighborhood. This called for some serious decision making. We were in the midst of adding more room for the beef cattle capacity. We reasoned, along with our neighbors, the offer was too good to pass up. It was a three year installment sale that gave us three years rent for one dollar per year.

That same year a dairy farm sale ad in Lebanon County caught our attention. It was a 106 acre farm, with a new barn equipped for 48 cows and another free stall barn on the property. It had a large stone house with oil heat and a new kitchen. After making several trips to look it over, along with my dad and Ruth's parents, we were ready for the sale day which took place on Thanksgiving Day, 1960. That day we signed another deed, after being greeted by several of the neighbors who welcomed us to the neighborhood.

We were on our way home that afternoon with a lot of varied thoughts and questions to be answered. The dairy barn was under quarantine until September, 1961 because of a brucellosis infection in the cattle. A few other factors influenced our thinking regarding a move to Lebanon County for the family at this time. We were giving our children the choice of finishing the last two years of high school at Lancaster Mennonite School if they so desired. Norma Jean was already driving our 1957 Chevy nine-passenger station wagon, transporting a number of other students from our area to LMS. We were also sharing responsibilities for caring for my invalid mother. Considering these conditions, we hired Amos Martin to serve as our herdsman, and his family moved into the farm house on September 1, 1961.

Soon thereafter two tractor trailer loads of cows and springing heifers almost filled the barn. Christ Erb, a local cattle dealer, and I had gone to Canada to purchase these registered Holsteins. We started shipping milk to Lehigh Valley Co-op in September, 1961. In 1962 we purchased a neighboring farm of 54 acres. This gave us another house for additional help. Together we enjoyed a good working relationship until October 1967, when the Martin family moved on.

Our son Jay, who was now married and had a young family, moved into the small farm to give dairy farming another chance. Jay had a handicap. Cow hair, hay dust and chicken feathers caused a persistent allergy problem. He gave the dairy farm a one-year try and was looking at other options. We didn't blame him. He became a long distance truck driver and is doing that to this day.

Lester Tice and family followed the Martin family on the farm. Around this time we built a double six milking parlor and enlarged the milking herd. We soon needed two full time men plus some family help from the Tices. We added two silos: a 25x65 haylage unit and a 20x70 high moisture corn unit. These were added to the 24x70 stave unit used for corn silage that had been there. Custom operators filled the silos.

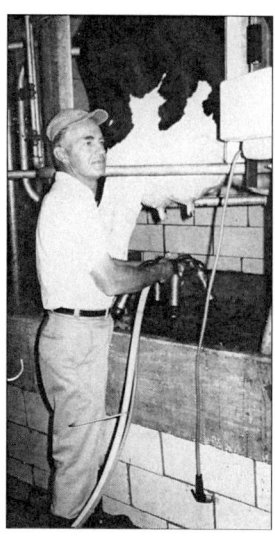 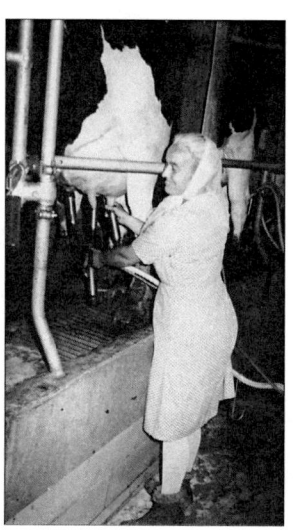

Ruth and I helped milk every other Sunday evening, giving one of the men time off. During the week I also filled in so that each man had one day off. This continued until September, 1978, when I offered to sell the cows to Lester Tice at a price below market value if he was interested. He refused. So on September 8, 1978 we had a milking herd dispersal, selling 140 cows, and we kept 100 heifers to be sold over the next two years. That year, Calvin Zimmerman, an aggressive young man, and his wife Thelma, rented both farms. He bought a number of cows at our sale. Calvin also rented some of our farm equipment until March 11, 1980, at which time we sold the farm equipment. By 1990 they bought the dairy farm and in 1996 they also bought the small farm. This brought our involvement in Lebanon County to a close. It was an interesting and challenging and adventurous experience. We also gained some new friends in that community.

CHAPTER EIGHTEEN

My Spiritual Growth

"Now I lay me down to sleep. I pray thee Lord my soul to keep. If I should die before I wake, I pray thee Lord my soul to take. And this I ask for Jesus sake. Amen." "The Angels are watching o'er me. All night, all night, the Angels are watching o'er me."

The first was my prayer and the second quote was my song. These routine, profound thoughts were foundational teachings to start me on my spiritual journey.

A lovely woman named Fannie Longenecker, a little older than my mother, was my Primary Sunday school teacher. She had a beautiful smiling face and loved each little boy and girl as her own children. I heard Bible stories in the Sunday school class and sang "Jesus Loves Me" and other children's songs. After the class period we gathered in the main auditorium and the Sunday school superintendent would review the lesson with the children's classes. One Sunday each quarter, there was a Temperance lesson. We talked about not smoking or drinking. When I was about 7 or 8 years old my Uncle Monroe Garber had the review for the Temperance lesson. I had a question for him. I raised my hand and asked, "Uncle Monroe, do you think it is right to raise tobacco?" I took him completely by surprise. He thought a bit and answered, "Well, Ruth, why don't you ask your daddy that question when you get home?" That satisfied me. Little did I know what a controversial question that was among the Mennonite farmers in our neighborhood during those years.

I remember asking my daddy what they used tobacco for. His answer usually was that they made fly spray out of it, called Black Leaf 40. This became a question among the young people, as we meditated on the thought, "If it is wrong to smoke, it is also wrong to grow it." But what was the alternative?

Mother did not read a lot of Bible stories to us, but the fact that she taught us to enjoy reading books and poetry helped me to be aware of good literature. I realized there were hidden meanings and lessons we could learn from reading other peoples' thoughts. When I was 10 to 12 years of age, I enjoyed hearing a good sermon and I started to take messages seriously. I began to realize I was born a sinner and needed a

Savior. The winter of 1934, Bro. John S. Hess had a two-week series of evangelistic meetings at the Bossler Mennonite Church. He had a kindly voice and I felt convicted of being of a sinful nature. I wanted to go to heaven when I died. After the service on Christmas Eve, 1934, my Sunday school teacher, another Fannie Longenecker, came to me and wondered if I was ready to accept Jesus as my Savior. I broke into tears and said "Yes." I was soon to be 12 years of age when I gave my name to the evangelist, indicating that I had accepted the Lord as my Savior. A burden rolled off my mind. When we got home in the kitchen, I thought the lights were brighter than before. Spiritual light entered my mind and my heart was cleansed from sin. Now I could pray and know "If I should die, the Lord would take my soul to be with Him!"

I had a series of instruction classes before the class of 8 or 10 young people were baptized by our bishop, Noah Risser. The following year my life was changed to becoming a big girl. Mother made cape dresses for me. I wore a big, white head covering and long, dark silk stockings. I remember being 13 years old when I got a new spring coat. It was pretty long for me. I picked out some dress shoes from the Sears catalogue. They had heels like my mother wore. I stood in front of the mirror in the guest room and admired myself. I was growing up and looked nice.

My Sunday school teacher was John Heistand. He made our

lessons very interesting by giving us a study book with blanks to fill in. I found passages of scripture that had interesting hidden meanings, such as, "The latchet of whose shoes I am unworthy to unloose." That interested me.

The spring of 1936 our family moved to New Danville. Wearing a dress with a cape, which was an extra piece of fabric over my chest and back, intended to preserve modesty, and a belt around my waist to keep it in place, was not the style for the girls in that new school. There were no other "plain" girls at Harmony Hall School. I discovered people liked me even if I did not dress like the other girls at school. The next year, Mother thought I looked nice as I started junior high school with my three new cape dresses. I was thankful for the 3 or 4 other "plain" girls in my high school class. I suppose I learned to have more tolerance for other minority groups as God brought them into my life.

The churches in our Lancaster Conference started having a young person write an essay on a given subject to be read at the Sunday evening meetings. I remember reading a few of these. One was on "Keeping the Sabbath Day Holy." Daddy helped me by suggesting some scriptures and thoughts to use. I read it at the Landisville Mennonite Church.

When I was 17 years old the deacon came to our house on a Saturday evening with an unusual request. He said there was a girl about my age who went to a neighboring mission church. She was in a class of young folks who were planning to be baptized the next morning. However, she did not have a cape dress to wear because her mother did not make dresses. This was a requirement for applicants for baptism. He wondered if I would have a dress for her to wear.

Mother had just finished making a new dress for me. I was looking forward to wearing it to church the next morning. I had only one dress which I was wearing on Sundays that season. It was very exciting for me to have another new dress. Mother put the question to me. After some deep deliberation and consideration of the blessing it would be to the girl and to me, I finally gave my consent to let my new dress be given for such a worthy cause.

My dress code was governed mostly by the bishop's strict observance of our interpretation of the Church Discipline in our daily life and practice. Of course, the deacon in our church helped him carry out the rules. One time our deacon suggested to my mother that I really should not be wearing brown shoes to school, as black would be more modest. This time Mother let me continue wearing brown shoes regardless of the deacon's suggestion.

As I began dating, the young couples would congregate on Sunday evenings wherever we thought the majority of our friends were going. It was always at one of the churches and usually there was a popular evangelist or Bible teacher giving the message. In retrospect I found these faithful servants of God very helpful in forming my convictions on morals and obedience to church discipline.

We also had a chance to see and meet a lot of other young people in these church settings. Actually, it was at these meetings that Elmer was noticing me. He had another young fellow show him where I lived before he came to see me.

After Elmer and I were dating we discussed with other young couples subjects such as, "Why is it customary for our acquaintances to get married and generally take up the same occupations as our parents had?" We lived where they did and went to the same churches. Little did we realize what effect the current World War II would have on these traditions. Our generation and the next generation definitely changed these customs. Young people in the next generation went into Voluntary Service and IW, which was alternate service for conscientious objectors who opposed military service. This scattered our own families and I could begin to see the value in voluntary service in mission projects and other work far from home.

There were summer Vacation Bible Schools and Sunday evening children's meetings in some mission churches where I accepted responsibilities in teaching. After we were married, our seven children took a lot of my time. I needed to daily commit our children and their care to God, who promised to give us wisdom when we felt our need. We depended on Him for direction each day. Elmer and I determined before we got married that we would have a meaningful Bible reading and prayer time after our breakfast each morning. Elmer always read the suggested daily scripture reading in our Sunday school quarterly, and we took turns leading in prayer. Hearing our praise and petitions from day to day gave us a focus for our spiritual life. God has blessed this time with His presence and to this day it is a commitment we would not want to change or leave out of our schedule.

As a young man, Elmer had a conviction against raising tobacco. After his dad bought the farm on Charlestown Road, Elmer got permission from his father to raise belladonna, a plant used to make medicine, instead of having any share of profit from the tobacco crop for a year or two. A few years later Elmer converted the tobacco shed into a three-story chicken house. He had baby chicks in the old summer house, the meadow house, and in the converted pig pen.

When our youngest child, Vera, was 3 years old, I was asked to teach a class of young girls in Sunday school at Millersville Mennonite Church. Elmer and I were both members of this church ever since we were married. Elmer was Superintendent of the Sunday school for eight years, after which he taught Sunday school also. I enjoyed teaching the girls. They were old enough to give their own thoughts. I continued teaching girls and young women for 30 years. There were about 10 years after that when I was a pupil in a class. When I was about 75 years old, I was asked to again teach the ladies my age and older. I thoroughly enjoyed these teaching years. I recognized that I needed to have my lunch basket filled before I could share the Bread of Life with others. My father often said, "You are not a good teacher until you find each student participating with a thought of their own. It takes discernment and patience to allow this to happen."

The neighborhood ladies' Bible study that Emma Moeller and I started in 1965 was part of me. It stretched my social circle. There were numerous denominations represented, I being the only Mennonite in the group of between six and nine ladies. It blessed me in ways that gave friendship a special meaning through the years. We learned to know God and each other more intimately as we shared our faith. We helped each other through prayer as we journeyed through the years of child rearing, as well as the children leaving home and when some of the husbands died. I thank God for that experience too.

I have read the Bible through several times. The first time was from the King James Version. In the King James I underscored the verses that had special spiritual meaning to me, with reference to God's message to me personally. In the Living Bible Translation, I underscored the times when God spoke to me in first person. I received new insights. It was easy to understand and get the picture of the settings and happenings. The Bible is my workbook. I have made many notations through the years as I was impressed with special thoughts given by ministers or teachers. I enjoy taking notes as outlines are shared.

When I read the New International Version, I tried something new. As I read it page by page and broke it down to one column at a time, I always looked for one emphasis in that column. I looked for the exchange between God and man. I tried to see the progression of God's relationship with man and man's response to God all the way through the 66 books of the Bible. I noticed God is in complete control of all creation and has given man the privilege of choice. In some columns God speaks or acts and in others man is responding, either for Him or against Him. Satan has the extreme opposite power from God's, but God has proven Himself to be the only power greater than Satan's. Jesus, God's Son, has represented that power of God on earth and the Holy Spirit dwells within us to give to us the same power of God.

This project took me three years to complete. I have a notation above each column in the entire Bible and it has been the most gratifying experience in my personal Bible study. It gave me direction for my spiritual life and filled my heart with thanksgiving for what God has done for mankind. I am

His child and He loves me. My decisions concerning how I dress have become more relaxed. Our witness to the world is more important than the clothes we wear. I want to be observed as a Christian who is Mennonite by choice.

There is a quote our family has picked up from my mother: "It will give something!" Whether inviting folks home from church for a meal, family stopping for a visit, or unexpected farm hands at the table, this quote is fitting for them all. A meal of some kind could be spread before our special guests with hungry appetites.

When I compare this to the unexpected needs in my spiritual life, I am amazed to realize how profoundly this quote fits my search for inner strength, and support for meeting the needs of my extended family, friends and acquaintances. "It will give something!"

In times of illness, family moving far away, divorce, death, loneliness or despair, I have found God close enough to me that I can find comfort and joy in some thought or song. I depend on Him. He will be forever faithful. Praise God! II Chronicles 16:9, "For the eyes of the Lord run to and fro throughout the whole earth, to show himself strong on behalf of those whose heart is loyal to Him." Isaiah 25:1 expresses my prayer. "O Lord, you are my God; I will exalt you and praise your name, for in perfect faithfulness you have done marvelous things; things planned long ago."

Elmer's newly crafted library shelves in the library at Millersville Mennonite Church, 1997. L-R: Eldon Nafziger, Elmer Rohrer, Janessa Charles, Rita Bleacher, Judy Harnish, Mary Deiter, Arlene Leaman and Cleon Huber.

John Huber, designer, and Bishop Abram Charles helped with the library installation.

CHAPTER NINETEEN

Church Life

Having given my heart to the Lord in my youth, I soon learned to lean not on my own understanding, but to seek His help. "Lead on, dear Father, lead on." This seemed to be very evident when teaching classes of upper-teen-age boys. My goal was to have each one respond to a thought or a question at least once that period, and sometimes take a turn teaching the lesson. It was when remembering that teaching experience that one of these boys expressed appreciation for that experience. He said it gave him confidence to accept and enjoy teaching a class at his church at a later date.

I think of the time in 1965, when the congregation was considering some extensive renovations and there was some dissension among us. Imagine the joy I felt, as chairman of the building committee, when Pastor Landis Shertzer was the first of the volunteers to arrive on the starting day of the project. He made the comment to me, "I did not vote in favor of this project, but the congregation did, and so I am here to help." That project went through to completion with a very good relationship among us.

Beginning about a year later and over the next few years, there was a breach in our church body relationships. Our bishop left our church and a number of other members went with him to start another congregation. Needless to say, relationships were broken and much healing was needed. In April 2001, our Bishop Abram Charles, "a pursuer of peace," called a meeting for healing relationships. He invited anyone to come who felt this need. A forgiving spirit prevailed at this time among the folks who gathered for this occasion. I was asked to give some thoughts of our journey through those years and I am including my story as it was given at that time.

"In the Throes of a Dilemma"

(difficult decisions)

I've been through the pains of a mini dilemma this week, trying to condense my thoughts into a 5 minute story. I'm doing something new lately. I'm attempting to use the computer. I find I must follow the rules. At times I get disgusted with that thing. I can't talk to it. I can't change its mind. It's been programmed and I need to abide. Humans are different from machines.

We need relationships. When pressed into a mold, a rebellious spirit is apt to develop. Good relationships cannot be legislated.

As Ruth and I were growing up we experienced a variety of leaders in our congregations. Some led with a sensitive and gentle spirit of love and compassion. Some were rigid and firm, expecting immediate compliance. Nevertheless we both experienced growth in our relationship with Christ. We felt fulfilled in our service for God and the Church.

Later in our married life there were changes in church leadership. We sensed an over-emphasis on the demands of the legalistic rules and regulations. This was cause for concern. Such a church atmosphere even made us feel uncomfortable to invite the unsaved to our services.

I believe this dilemma carries an extra load for me. I was in the "lot" when the leader who left our church was ordained. There is an unwritten expectation that those who were in the lot together will be especially loyal and supportive to the one who was selected. I struggled with knowing if that loyalty should supersede my personal convictions at that point.

The focus of this dilemma became sharper as our children were considering baptism and later marriage. Our children were finding evidence of the Christian walk in the lives of people who were not Mennonites. Ruth and I also appreciated Christians of other faiths and enjoyed fellowship with them. This created an even greater conflict for us. Do we fully follow leaders with rigid rules? Do we demand our children to also comply? Or do we trust our children to be sensitive to the Spirit's leading in their lives? They needed to own the decisions they were making.

It hurt us to see the demands and expectations that were made of our children. We understood why some families were leaving. We keenly felt the loss of these friends from our fellowship. However, we realize many of them made significant contributions in the life of other congregations.

Our children learned to comply with the rules to a degree, along with some hurts and misunderstandings. As one graphic example, we saw our daughter, Sue, leaving for college with a somewhat rebellious spirit. We entrusted her to the Lord in much prayer, not knowing what influence would be the strongest in her life. Months later she had a spiritual awakening. Her roommate was influential in challenging her spiritual life. She wrote home telling us she appreciated what we tried to do and say, but she needed to experience the Spirit's leading for herself. The letters that followed showed evidence of much spiritual growth.

In retrospect, we see evidence of God graciously leading our children, in spite of negative experiences, each having their own love for the Lord and the Church. At this point in time we have moved on. God is blessing our small cluster of believers here at Millersville. However, there is still pain in remembering the past.

Oh, that we could identify with Jabez, as recorded in I Chronicles 4:9 and 10, and seek with earnest hearts that God would bless Millersville Mennonite Church indeed. And that God would heal us of our pain. May God grant to us our request, as He granted Jabez his request.

(In 2015 the Millersville congregation is blessed to have Wes and Millie Penner serving as co-pastors. We are enjoying a spirit of warm love and see evidence of spiritual renewal.)

In 1997 the congregation again considered making some changes. The library needed to be at a more prominent place. Our deacon, John Henry Harnish, asked me if I would consider making the desk, shelving and cabinets for the new library. I assured him there would not be any wood costs involved if I could use the cherry lumber I had on hand. John Huber drew up the plans and also sprayed on the finish. I also knew that John would be a good consultant when I needed one. I added a plank top cherry library table to the plan.

And there was another involvement I had at church. My great grandfather, Rudolph S. Herr, was a charter member of the Millersville Mennonite cemetery board, followed by my grandfather Rudolph L. Herr. He was followed by my father, Elmer B. Rohrer. I also served over 20 years on the same cemetery board.

An early Eby reunion when the grandmas sat on rocking chairs.

A happy family vacation to Skyline Drive, Virginia. From left: Mother, Jay,
Ruth, Marian, Jean and Anna Martha.1939

CHAPTER TWENTY

Family Vacations
A Change of Pace

A vacation is a change from the regular routine of things. This was true through the years in varied lengths of time and varied distances from home. According to my memory, when I was a child our family reunions were like a vacation to our family. Around the 4th of July we went to the Eby Reunion. My grandmother Garber was an Eby. Her brother, Henry Eby lived on the Eby homestead, near Mount Joy, PA. My mother would pack a picnic lunch that morning. She would be sure to have a cake baked for that day. She would squeeze out some lemons and take along the juice with plenty of sugar. We needed to hurry to get to this gathering by noontime. It was said that the Ebys were always on time but the Garbers were apt to be arriving in the nick of time. There was much to do to prepare for this picnic.

As we drove those 15 miles to Mount Joy, all of us stretched our necks to find the lane that went in to those farm buildings. The house was a large, limestone home with a big porch. Aunt Annie kept the lawn immaculate. We drove between the barns and then down a grassy lane where the hay or barley had just been harvested. This lane took us to the meadow and on down toward the Chickies Creek. Oh yes, there were the people sitting on blankets with their babies. The older aunts and uncles brought a few chairs of various kinds. There was the private place made by hanging large heavy blankets between trees next to the meadow fence. A makeshift toilet seat was placed in there year after year. That is where the girls could change into their bathing suits after dinner to go swimming in the creek.

Oh, it was so exciting to see our first cousins and second cousins around our ages. Some of the uncles would help the boys go fishing down along the creek. They brought worms along and an extra rod or two.

But we can't forget the meal. There was a large stone crock provided to mix the lemonade. Each jar of lemon juice and sugar was poured into the crock as a certain amount of water was added from a milk can filled at the spring near the house. It made the best lemonade! We all had our tin cups along for this treat. The mothers and grandmothers spread their table-cloths in a long row on the grass, being careful there were no fresh cow pies underneath. Then the men would bring the car seats that were removable from the automobiles and place them on each side of the tablecloths. Of course, the children sat on the blanket if there was only room for the adults on the seats. Some of the older grandmothers even sat on chairs at the sides, and the food was handed up to them. One of the uncles or a grandpa would give thanks and ask a blessing on this meal. We would sing a hymn before the food was served.

As the picnic baskets were emptied these tablecloths were filled with sandwiches, red beet eggs, potato salad, freshly made apple sauce made from the early harvest apples and any fruit that was available in jars or fresh from the trees. The amazing part of the meal was the moment the cakes were being passed. Each family brought a cake and each cake was passed down the line and up again on the other side. It was like a parade. We could take as many pieces as we could eat. But we needed to eat whatever we took. Nothing was to be wasted.

The children needed to wait an hour after the meal to go in the water. This was our one chance in the year to go swimming. Actually, some of us only waded up to our armpits because we never had a chance to learn to swim. This part of the creek was reserved for the ladies and girls. The men and boys walked down the stream and around the corner quite a way before they got into the stream. You see, they had no swim suits and they were allowed to take off their clothes down there and swim naked. At least that is what I heard from my big girl cousins.

About four o'clock in the afternoon a truck would appear with three large ice cream freezers wrapped in heavy blankets. When the men were finished pitching quoits (sort of like horseshoes, but round) and the children all had clothes on again and the women had finished talking about problems with their babies and the older folks had shared about their aches and pains and all the latest news about the relatives was shared, it was time to get out the ice cream plates and spoons for a good serving of homemade ice cream. Each family needed to give one dollar to pay for this treat. That meant the small families could help the large families enjoy this specialty without making it a hardship for anyone.

When the last goodbyes were said and all the seats were back in the cars and the water cans and the freezers were loaded on the truck again, we hurried home to the farm to finish up the evening work at the barn. We had had a wonderful vacation day.

This amazing treat was repeated in August when we would go to the Garber Reunion. This was on a smaller scale because it was only the Simon and Fannie Garber family. It was held at various homes of the uncles and aunts; each family took a turn from year to year. Uncle Henry's had a large lawn at their farm near Mount Joy. Their daughter, my oldest cousin Catherine, went to Africa as a missionary after she married John Leatherman. They were some of the first missionaries sent from the Eastern Mennonite Board of Missions in the Lancaster Conference. This was very impressive to the younger cousins. It seemed like quite a spiritual adventure to me. We would excitedly read their mimeographed personal letters when they were circulated bi-monthly by mail.

At this reunion Grandma Garber made a large boiler container of chicken corn soup. The corn was cut off ears that were grown in her garden and the chicken was cut up from some of Grandpa's special flock. Grandma knew how to make rivals, adding an egg to a large handful of flour. She mixed the egg in the flour with her hand and dropped the rivals into the very hot soup and stirred the soup 'til it boiled just long enough to thicken the broth. Then we would each get our bowl filled out there in the yard or wherever we met that year. Again we had homemade ice cream in the afternoon. The cousins played hide and seek or had a peanut scramble and talked and laughed together 'til it was time to go home.

There was one other reunion the first Monday in August, called the Social Reunion. This was a group of about 100 people. The adults were all acquaintances of my parents. They had been friends since before they were married. They all had memories of their courtship days and earlier. This is where I learned to know other young girls who were Mennonites from as many as 25 miles away. There was another couple from this group, Elam and Elizabeth Stauffer, who were among the first missionaries to Africa, along with John and Catherine. I was convinced that God wanted Mennonites to take the Gospel to foreign countries.

When we were little girls living at Bossler Corner, we had the chance to go to Grandpa Herr's for a week at a time. Mother would pack the leather grippe which was a type of suitcase with snaps and a handle on the top. My sister and I went together in the summer time. Grandpa and Grandma Herr or our Great Uncle Ira and Great Aunt Anna Herr would come to our home and we went along with them to New Danville or Millersville. We stayed 4 days at one place and 3 days at the other. We loved being at Uncle Ira's because they lived in the town of Millersville. They had a front porch with a swing on chains hanging from the ceiling. On those summer evenings we would sit on the porch and Aunt Anna would read stories and nursery rhymes to us. She had no children and we felt her love and attention as if we were her very own. They did have a girl, Laura Carrigan, who they raised as their own. Laura was fond of us too. We would watch her dress up for her dates on Sunday evening. She was like an aunt or big cousin and we loved her too.

I remember that the Pequea trolley went by Uncle Ira's sidewalk. One summer we got on the trolley and rode from Millersville, across the Conestoga Creek and on down to Grandpa Herr's home, where we got off the trolley above the yard. We had to go down some steps that Grandpa made to get to their house. Grandpa had a garden up near the trolley tracks and that is where I helped him plant sweet corn. He would dig the hole with his hoe and he said, "Drop 3 kernels in the hole. One for the crow, one that won't grow and one to grow tall and give us an ear or two of corn." He loved his garden and I loved helping him.

It wasn't exactly "vacation," but it was a change of pace, as we grew older and lived across the meadow from Grandpa and Grandma Herr. We girls helped Grandpa cut asparagus for his customers. We had a knife to cut it off and a bucket to put it in. He had an acre or two and needed some helpers. After it was cut we dipped large handfuls of it in a tub of water to wash off the soil that stuck on it. Then we sorted it on the wooden table, according to the size of the stalks. We went from small to tall. Then we picked up a handful from one end and weighed out a pound which was all about one size. We put a rubber band around it. We kept that scale busy as we worked all forenoon before it got too hot out in the field. We girls earned a little money that way when I was about 14 or 15 years old.

Until the age of 15, these were the only family vacation days that I knew about. One day Mother said we were going to DuPont Gardens, now called Longwood Gardens, for the day. We packed a lunch and our family walked around those lovely, manicured grounds and through the glass greenhouses. The orchids and other exotic plants fascinated me. I remember being a little embarrassed to be walking with this large family of seven. I was getting to be a big girl now and so I stayed back about 30 feet from the rest as we walked along. Did I want to be a little independent or was I getting a little contrary about staying in a group?

The next year Mother planned a trip to Skyline Drive in Virginia. We stayed in little tourist cabins for 2 nights. How exciting to make ourselves at home in these little doll-like houses with a bed, dresser and a little bathroom in each house.

Our family took a few other trips before I was engaged to be married to Elmer. We went to the World's Fair in New York City and to the ocean for 2 nights in Avalon, New Jersey. One day Mother said, "You know, Ruth, you won't be able to go with us on any trips after you get married." I think she aimed to put me to the test. Would I be satisfied to leave my family and cleave only to my husband? Oh, yes, I would rather be with Elmer than go on a trip with the family! I loved my sweetheart. I believe Mother thought she would miss me too, when they took a trip after I got married.

As our children grew up, Elmer and I felt vacations were very important for the family. We usually had farm helpers that could milk the cows and take care of the chickens and eggs for a short time. So we would go for a day or two or a week at a time to places like the Philadelphia Zoo, the ocean, to the Smoky Mountains, to Laurelville Camp, to Canada and to mountain cabins at Wheelerville or Bellville. These stories are in my journals that I wrote as we traveled along unfamiliar scenery. I recorded some of the interesting comments made by our young family in those journals. There are two of these trips added to these pages as I recorded them in 1959 and 1962.

Our children were hard workers on the farm. They would have many stories of their own, telling of the work that was cut out for each of them. Their school days and days with their friends from church and times shared with their grandparents and cousins will fill a book that they can each write some day.

When the children were older, Elmer and I were privileged to take bus trips to Moosenee and Prince Edward Island. We enjoyed the fellowship of the group tours, but we preferred the trips where we could go at our own pace. In 1982 we went to the Canadian Rockies and Alaska in a Winnebago motor home with my siblings, Marian and Jay, and their spouses. Jay had married Lois Leaman in 1952. At the office at Denali

National Park, we read that our visit occurred on the best day of the year for viewing Mount McKinley (Denali), the highest mountain in North America. The six of us enjoy being together from time to time doing a variety of activities.

We also have travel journals from trips to Honduras, Guatemala, Mexico and areas of the U.S. We have always enjoyed traveling together, and as our family scattered, we had plenty of places to go to visit them. Our children surprised us with a gift to mark our 50th wedding anniversary when they arranged a 12-day tour of Europe in 1994, organized through *Country Magazine*. We later had a four-week visit to Europe with Norman and Arlene Leaman in 2001, when we were invited to attend the wedding of Jolene Harnish in Germany. Jolene was a friend from our church.

We visited Denali National Park in Alaska on an exceptionally clear day, so we had an excellent view of the whole mountain.

L-R: Elmer, Ruth, Jay and Lois Garber, and Marian and Henry Leaman.

CHAPTER TWENTY-ONE

Other Friends And Activities

As I look back over my life, there are other people and events I must mention. Grandpa Kiefer is one who each of the family remembers. When we were first married, I heard a loud voice talking with Elmer near the barn. When he came to the house, he explained to me that it was Mr. Frank Kiefer, who lived about a half mile up the road. He said I should not be afraid of him, even if he talks so loud and seems to be scolding about something. His wife had died around that time. He was keeping dogs and monkeys in some cages in the back of his barn. According to the collective information in the neighborhood, he would go to the Acme grocery stores and pick up the day old breads and buns and sweet rolls to feed to his animals. He had a gruff voice and was usually out of sorts about something, it seemed to us. However, as we learned to know the man, he enjoyed talking with us.

I did not get to relate to Mr. Kiefer very much until our family started to grow larger. First, he talked about the amount of food it takes to feed a family. He had five children, all of whom were gone from his home by that time. When we had about four or five little ones, he started to stop at our gate and told the kids in our yard to come out to his truck for some of his sweet rolls etc. He would say, "Here, eat this. You're hungry; you gotta' have something to eat." Then he started bringing bananas, fig bars and cookies that were outdated. He started blowing his horn as he came up the road toward the house. Then he would stop and bellow, "Where's Mom?" Then when the children had gathered around him at the back of his half ton truck, he would say in his loud voice, "Tell your mom to come out!" I needed to stop whatever I was doing and go up the six steps to the roadside and he would say, "Here, take these rolls; there is nothing wrong with them. It takes a lot of food to feed such a family."

When I was pregnant with number six or seven, he stopped by Elmer along the road and said, "No wonder the school taxes are high." But regardless of his loud mannerisms, I could tell he loved our family. He called himself "Grandpa Kiefer" and wanted the children to call him that. He would actually stop sometimes on Sunday mornings and watch me dress the little ones for Sunday school. Since our bathroom was downstairs, I also kept the children's clothes in the kitchen area. One time we came home from a family vacation and had an enormous pile of dirty laundry near the washer and dryer in our kitchen. He came storming into the kitchen and said, "Lady, I pity you from the bottom of my heart." He could not believe that I thought it was so wonderful to have spent 6 or 7 days away from home, even if it did give a mountain of laundry.

Sometimes Mr. Kiefer would ask for a homemade pie. I usually made an extra pie for him. We gave him strawberries from our garden. I gave him corn fritter batter one time. My parents gave him the perfect treat. They invited Grandpa Kiefer, his daughter and his son to their home for a meal, along with our family. When he was in the hospital, toward the end of his life, Elmer and I went to visit him and prayed with him. He was of the Catholic faith and I believe God knew he loved Him. Mr. Keifer expressed his appreciation for our interest in his well being.

There were other families that became good friends with us. They were the people who lived on the other side of our farm house. The husbands helped Elmer with the farm work; the children played together and we ladies shared the subjects that were dear to our hearts.

Emma Moeller, who was one of the first neighbors in the new

Bowling Green development, became one of my closest friends in the community. She and I started a Bible study group that touched the lives of many different neighbor ladies from the year 1960 to 2000. Chie Layman and Ann Adams were part of that group and are still my friends in 2015. We get together once each month for a meal and sharing time. Our cultures are quite different and we have enjoyable conversations as we share our Christian faith and experiences.

I was part of a Bible study group in our neighborhood for more than 40 years. This picture includes my friends Emma, Chie, Gladys, Nancy, me and Ann.

I learned to find satisfaction and happiness in volunteering my time in various endeavors. Elmer generally encouraged me to do the things that I felt called to do. I tried to make time for these extra opportunities for service and was challenged by the responsibilities of serving and leading committees. The Homebuilders project of sending literature to folks with special spiritual needs took some of my time. I helped to organize birthday parties for the Harrisburg State Hospital patients. My Great Uncle Ira Herr was the first Treasurer of the Millersville Children's Home many years ago. It was meaningful to me to be Secretary of the Board when the Children's Home was reorganized as the Millersville Youth Village.

Black Rock Retreat at Quarryville took a lot of my time when I was on that Board. Being in charge of the kitchen at Black Rock Retreat for 2½ years was the ultimate fulfillment for me as a volunteer, next to my homemaking responsibilities. I had the feeling that all the people I served were my special guests. Many wonderful volunteer ladies and some men gave many hours to help in meal preparation for weddings, retreats and other church-related activities. I remember many good times from my volunteer work at Black Rock Retreat, even to this day. I felt so inadequate for these responsibilities, but I found that God was so real to me and helped as it says in II Corinthians 12:9: "My strength is made perfect in weakness."

I was on the first Church Council for Millersville Mennonite Church, as Fellowship and Service Department Chairperson. Sewing Circle and the Columbia Re-Uzit Shop were other volunteering days that filled my time and gave volunteering special meaning.

There were some new experiences in my life as I got older. When I was 65 years of age, Elmer was starting to play golf and he encouraged me to try it too. So I got some clubs and we spent some pleasant times together on the golf course. We also played with other friends on several different golf courses. The one exciting time was with our granddaughter, Becky, in Nebraska. I remember actually hitting a robin that time. The bird tumbled around a bit, and then took off. I remember telling Elmer that time that "I got a birdie!" That would be a coveted feat for some of us amateur golfers.

Snorkeling with Sue and Duane in Mexico was a thrill. The life on the bottom of the Pacific Ocean was so impressive. I'm not a swimmer, but Sue helped me get onto a floating raft and put my face in the water with a snorkeling mask. Then she pushed me around in the water so I could see the beautiful fish and coral formations. In fact, the experience of visiting with them in the Mexican culture was a high spot in our lives. Seeing the lives that are so completely changed, when the people become believers in Jesus, is an experience we will never forget.

"Going to the Cabin." How sweet those words are as we re-

member the many times our family gathered there for summer fun and also special holiday gatherings. Elmer had the invitation in 1983 to join nine other men in a hunting camp named "William's Manor Retreat" in Lycoming County, PA.

The enlarged cabin on the property is big enough to accommodate 20 or more people, depending how much togetherness one wishes to tolerate. Its two bathrooms and long dining room tables are among the facilities that make it acceptable for gathering friends and families and for building many bonding memories. Through shuffleboard games, hiking, table games, eating and other activities we shared love and strengthened family ties. The grandchildren were in favor of spending Thanksgiving or Christmas holidays and summer vacations "at the cabin."

The computer was one of the most unbelievable inventions in my life experiences. I feel so privileged to have a laptop computer of my own. To connect with our family by email in the

The folks from the Sunday school classes Elmer and I taught spent a weekend with us at the cabin annually for about 18 years.

matter of pressing a key just makes life so convenient. Nancy gets the credit for encouraging me when the idea was new. Our children shared the cost of this luxury. I did not think I could learn this skill at my age. But it happened, as I was brave enough to follow some instructions. Nancy likes to tell one story about when she was helping me learn to use the computer. She says, "I told Mother I think she's far enough along that she can find some answers by going to 'Help' on the email program. That night, about 10:30, Mother called me and said, 'I'm in Help and I can't get out!'." I am thankful I can put this story on this machine and print it from there.

Spending our winters in Florida gave a new dimension to our social and spiritual life. We developed new friendships with people from many different states and Canada. Singing with

the Bahia Vista Estates Chorus was one of my pleasant experiences. Arnold Moshier, who led the music department at
Lancaster Mennonite High School when our girls went there,
led our choir and I felt so privileged to sing in the group.
Playing shuffleboard with as many as 50 different players
was another fun surprise. Having Bible study with about 30
different ladies who also lived in Bahia Vista Estates was also
meaningful. We enjoyed eating fruit from our own orange
tree. Living double with Harry and Evelyn Rohrer (no rela-
tive) in a double wide mobile home two months of the year
not only cut the rent in half, but also gave us a new sense of
community living. Playing Crazy Black Rook became a very
popular pastime in the evenings. We would laugh and relax
for several hours at a time. Having time to read and write was
special for me. During those times I could meditate and remember the past, and think about the future. The visitors
that spent a few days or more with us were happy to know
someone who lives in this romanticized winter vacation land.
Our 15 winters in Sarasota were precious and enjoyable in
many ways.

Elmer has a hobby that has brought much pleasure to both of
us. He likes woodworking. He had the foresight to use an old
building that was on the neighboring Armstrong property
when they did not want it any longer. He tore it down and
built it up again on our property after we moved to 1270

Manor Blvd. His wood shop gave him many hours of satisfaction as he designed and made useful furniture and other special things. He cut the mature walnut and wild cherry trees from the fence lines of the Lebanon County farm and also from the farm at home. He got the wood sawed into boards and he dried it carefully for many years. He enjoyed making reproductions of antique furniture, such as the hall rack that my father hung his hat on when he dated my mother. He made about two dozen blanket chests. He made a settee for our living room, among other things. One big project was a walnut corner cupboard for our dining room. Elmer continues to work with wood in the shop at Landis Homes, where he builds Crokinole boards. He sells the game boards and gives the proceeds to Roca Blanca Missions, or donates the boards to fund-raising auctions.

We visited Sue and Duane in Mexico seven times over the past 25 years. Our most recent visit was in 2011, but this picture is from the early 1990s.

Ruth Writes

CHAPTER TWENTY-TWO

Illnesses And Miracles

I was 5 years old when I became very sick. Dr. Trichler from Elizabethtown came to our home. He was half way up the stairs when he could smell the odor coming from the bedroom where I was lying. He recognized the odor as diphtheria. He immediately turned around and hurriedly went to Marietta, where the Wythe Laboratories were located, to get the new toxin antitoxin drug. He got a large dose for me and smaller doses for the rest of the family so that they would stay immune to the dreaded disease. This was a new medication and it undoubtedly saved my life. I was so sick that I could not sit up to drink water. I can recall that Mother got the tiny toy teapot from the old child-size china set and I drank from the spout as it was held to my mouth. Since the disease was so contagious, Daddy was assigned to be my nurse and Mother stayed out of the room and took care of my two little sisters. That was a difficult time for my parents, and we thank God for delivery from that serious illness.

I had other childhood diseases, but I waited 'til I was a junior in high school to have the mumps. I missed two weeks of school until I was not quarantined any longer. I had a severe case of poison ivy when I was seven years old. My legs were covered with blisters and Mother used lots of cornstarch powder to cool them down. I have never had poison so badly since that time.

The summer of 1949 was a hard one for our family on the farm near Millersville. Our daughter, Norma Jean, contracted scarlet fever at four years of age. We all needed to be quarantined. Jay was a baby and our friend, Edith, was there to help me the day the doctor quarantined us. She needed to stay on the farm too. It was about that same time that Elmer was baling straw with a Wisconsin motor on the New Holland hay baler. As he rounded a corner in the field, some carbon from the exhaust escaped and flew into his eye. He was taken to the hospital. Upon examination the surgeon thought they would operate the next day. However, the next morning the doctor was amazed that the eye did not need surgery. We used medicated drops instead and soon the eye healed. Our family doctor said he would not have given a dime for that eye when he first saw it. Praise God for that miracle.

When Jay was about nine months old, he had a cold and some fever. He was in bed one afternoon, when I found him in convulsions. I remembered the time my brother had a seizure and Mother put a cold washcloth on his head and put his feet in warm water. So I quickly took Jay to the trough where we had running water in the kitchen and did the same. He had those seizures again that night and the doctor comforted me by saying he would soon be well again. I thank God he never had convulsions after that time.

When Jay was a toddler, he broke a milk bottle on the neighbor's porch. He had some glass in his mouth and I was afraid he may have eaten some. Dr. Musselman advised me to feed him some cotton mixed into mashed potatoes. He said the glass would stick to the cotton and he would pass it that way.

One day Jay swallowed a little axel from a toy tractor. The doctor said, "Just watch the potty. He will surely pass it." Sure enough, it did come straight on through and into the potty.

One day Nancy fell down the hay hole in the barn, onto a cement floor. I hurriedly took her to the doctor's office. The waiting room was full of patients. I sat there with my sleeping little pre-schooler, wondering if she had a concussion. By the time it was my turn, she was walking around, like normal. Nancy had an eye problem that did not go away. The doctor said she was wall-eyed. Her one eye drifted out and she needed surgery to tighten the muscles. She had surgery when she was six years old and again when she was nine years old.

I had a tachycardia heart problem through the years. At certain intervals, my heart would start beating very rapidly, up to 200 beats per minute. About five or ten minutes later, it would go back to a normal speed, leaving me feeling a bit weak, but I soon had my regular energy again. A few times the problem lasted for an hour or more. This condition occurred a couple of times, requiring hospitalization. When we were in Honduras, I was treated in the Tegucigalpa hospital. I started taking Digoxin daily after that and some years later I thought the Lord had healed me, so I stopped taking the medicine. A couple years after that, I had a very severe episode when my heart beat rapidly for about two hours. It took six weeks to regain my strength. The heart specialist advised me to take Digoxin every day as long as I live. I praise God I have never had an attack since that day.

There were other physical problems during the years that called for some routine surgeries. When I had the cesarean section operation for Nancy's birth, I was lying on the operating table. As they started giving me anesthesia, I suddenly saw the face of Christ so distinctly in the bright light. I knew He was there, guiding the surgeon. He said, "Lo, I am with you always, even unto the end of the world." Thank you, God, for your promise. Yes, Jesus has been with us. He is a very real presence in the time of trouble! I have learned to praise God for what is good and praiseworthy, and then trust Him for those things that we cannot change. He is Lord!

My parents were blessed with good health for many years. They did a lot of traveling in the United States, Canada, Central America and Europe. They made many new friends as they circulated among Christians in many parts of the world 'til they were in their late eighties. Mother gradually lost her strength after she had her fourth pacemaker inserted to help her heart. She and Daddy moved to the Mennonite Home for health care after Daddy suffered a severe stroke. They were nearly ninety years old at that time. Mother died on August 24, 1989, at 91 years of age, from congestive heart failure. Daddy died at age 92 from kidney failure, on January 28, 1991. Mother and Daddy were ready to leave this world for a much better one over yonder. Mother would many times say, "Oh, that will be glory for me," as she longed to be free from her discomforts in her worn out body. This song was sung at her funeral. "When by His grace we shall look on His face; that will be glory for me!" Jesus will be there for us to praise Him, some glad day, when we all get to Heaven. Praise God!!

We grieved the loss of my two youngest sisters. Jean was married to John Huang, from Taiwan, and lived in the Baltimore, MD area. She had multiple health problems and died on November 19, 2002. Anna Martha, whom we lovingly called "Ann," struggled with mental illness and tuberculosis throughout her adult years. Ann died on June 12, 2003.

The Garber family in the early 1980s.

Standing: Marian, Ann, Jay, Jean, Ruth

Seated: my parents, Clarence and Vera

Garber siblings and spouses in July, 2000. L-R: Elmer and Ruth Rohrer,
Henry and Marian Leaman, Anna Martha "Ann" Garber,
Lois and Jay Garber, Jean and John Huang.

When we converted the tobacco barn to a chicken house, we put in an elevator to carry the eggs to the basement from the first through third floors. The children helped with the chickens from an early age.

Here Jay helps with washing eggs, basket by basket.

CHAPTER TWENTY-THREE

Raising The Family

I would be remiss if I would not talk about the challenge of raising seven children. Yes, it was a challenge. Many times we needed to ask the Lord to give us wisdom and to lead us on. Did we treat them all alike? If you were to ask them that question, you may receive varied answers. We loved the challenge and we loved each one, as varied as they were. Ruth has given a very good coverage to this subject, as well as other subjects regarding the children in her part of this book. Our vacations together were memory builders. Sharing in the work, gathering and packing eggs, driving the tractors and gardening, are some more of the memory builders.

Those work experiences may have helped to develop the good work ethic that each of them now have. Yes, we worked, we played, we prayed together. There were times we cried together. I cannot remember a time when I counseled Jay about his conduct even as much as my dad told me, regarding the story of Joseph and Potiphar's wife, and how Joseph had a ready answer saying "How can I do this wicked thing and sin against God?" (Genesis 39:9b) Had I shared more intimately with Jay, it might have spared us some heartaches.

We do not get a second chance to raise our children. How thankful I am that we do have a heavenly Father that forgives my many short comings, as well as our children's short comings, to the point that unity and love abound, as we allow Him to lead on. There were times when I read John, chapter 17 and sense the bonds of love that were present between the Father and Son. Then Jesus relates the same bond with His disciples. Beyond that, He prays that we, too, may have that relationship.

There were years when Jay and I were not on the same page. We always maintained contact, but our relationship was not close. One day, when Ruth and I were visiting Jay and Jane in Montana, Jay and I took a walk in the Rocky Mountains. Jay said, "Dad, I want to show you the spot where I shot my elk." Yes, I was eager. As we stood there together, John 17:20 came to my mind. I was overwhelmed with the thought that Jesus' prayer was being answered in Jay and me. We again shared that common bond of love. And His was an ongoing prayer, even for our posterity as they come to faith in Him.

To me, this mountainside conversation was what I will call "a warm fuzzy moment." Even to this day, as we end our weekly phone conversations, I love hearing Jay say, "I love you Dad." In fact, as any one of our seven children end a conversation with "I love you Dad, (or Daddy)," it gives me a warm fuzzy moment.

I didn't grow up with that kind of demonstration of love. I remember seeing my dad greet other men at church with the "holy kiss," as was the practice in those days. Our church observed the practice described in Romans 16:16: "Greet one another with a holy kiss." At church, the men would kiss men as they shook hands, and women would kiss women as they greeted one another, but the practice was restricted to only those "of like precious faith." That meant that only other Mennonites of like practice were greeted with a kiss. So, our family kissed other people, but I don't remember getting kisses from my dad, or even from my mother, although it may be that my memory fails me in this regard. I never doubted my parents' love for me, but we didn't show one another love with hugs and kisses.

However, Ruth and I were free with hugs and kisses for our children. Goodnight kisses and farewell hugs and kisses were standard when they were young, and today our comings and goings usually include hugs and kisses. These demonstrations of love mean a lot to me.

By Spring 1956, we were a family of nine.

Arriving at Grandpa Garber's for Christmas

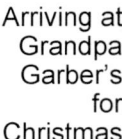

The girls are dressed for Uncle Bob and Aunt Lorraine's wedding.

Jay shows off his hunting trophy.

CHAPTER TWENTY-FOUR

Family Life Overview

"Nothing is more valuable than family, nor more worth our investment of patience and love, even if there are growing pains." This is a quote I came across in the "Better Homes and Gardens" magazine, by the Editor in Chief, Jean Lem-Mon.

I agree, even as Bishop David Thomas did. His children's play and even the destruction it caused meant more to him than his immaculate lawn, which the neighbor noticed they were tearing up. "I will grow grass later, after the children have grown up," he informed the neighbor.

Our babies entered our family in 11 years' time. Having seven children around the table by the time I was 33 years old was more of a challenge to me than any other responsibility I ever had before. I knew those were formative years for them and it would either make or break me.

One day Jay was looking very distraught. "I wish I had a brother," he said. "Well Jay, there are lots of boys who have only sisters. They have no brother," I reasoned with him. "Yes, but not so many!" he asserted.

Having a sister only 16 months younger wasn't quite close enough, in Nancy's opinion. She wanted a sister her age.

Nancy said one day, "I wish I had someone closer to my age in this family." Linda was only 17 months younger than she was. Nancy was not the oldest or the youngest. She was in the middle.

Vera was the youngest in the family. When I met friends along the way, they would thoughtlessly say, "Is this your baby?" She would immediately hide behind my skirt and feel too little to match the rest of the family.

One night I heard our six-year-old Nancy crying in her bedroom. Upon asking her what troubled her, she said, between sobs, "I am not your little girl." This statement I could not understand. But soon the realization dawned on me when I thought about the conversation I had with visitors the day before. Vera Ann was a baby and I was commenting to my friend that Nancy was the only one of the children that did not have the trademark dimple in her chin. All the rest had that dimple in their chin, but not Nancy. Yes, Nancy was a discerning little girl. This struck her as evidence that she did not belong. Oh! This is not what I meant! I hurriedly hugged her and explained the best that I could that she was, indeed, our treasured little girl.

Even more than I was aware of these problems, I am now fully aware that God must be praised for who these seven children became as adults. God was weaving the circumstances and our prayers for wisdom into a tapestry that now appears in beautiful shades of personalities and usefulness, for His glory. We did the best we knew at the time when decisions needed to be made. We made some poor judgments but God blessed our efforts. My policy was, "If it is not destructive, let them do it. If no one is getting hurt, let them enjoy their fun." I learned to talk with them and treat them like I would do to a friend or a friend's child. I tried to think how I would feel if someone spoke to me like I was talking to my child. I tried to show the child that the feelings of others are more important than their own selfish feelings.

I prayed about these kinds of challenges and many times felt inadequate to live up to my ideals. Disappointments came as

I realized my rules and ideas were not working. I needed God's miraculous works to allow these children to become the individuals He wanted them to become. And God is so faithful!

Norma Jean was not happy when friends came to see our new baby. For 2½ years she was our pride and joy. She declared she did not like her baby sister. I dropped to my knees that night and said, "Lord, I don't know how to handle this relationship problem." As our curly-headed Susie grew, she entertained everyone with her antics and became the perfect companion for her brother who was 16 months younger than she was. Jay soon passed her shorter stature in size.

Growing up on a farm gives children a variety of experiences. Elmer and I appreciated the help the children gave us. They mowed the lawn, pulled weeds in the garden, gathered eggs in the hen houses, cleaned and packed eggs in the egg cellar and drove the tractors for various daily and seasonal tasks. Saturday morning there was a list of cleaning jobs for the ones who did not need to pack eggs that day. There was tomato juice and applesauce to press through the sieve in canning season. The pile of sweet corn to husk and get into the freezer and the lima beans to hull for freezing were yearly summer routines. Everything tasted so good in the winter time, but at the time, the children did not fully realize these blessings were among the greatest advantages for living in the country.

There were neighbor children who knew the chores needed to be finished before our children could have time to play. Some had a chance to help and later they played in the barn, making tunnels with the hay bales, through which they crawled. At night there were sleep-outs in the meadow or on top of the broiler house roof. There were neighbor boys who helped to load the hay bales and were rewarded with large bowls of fresh strawberry shortcake for dinner.

The girls each had the opportunity to sew and play the piano. Some took more interest in these activities than others. One of the sweetest sounds to my ears was when Vera took flute lessons. That music is so clear and melodious. I never tired of hearing it.

Jay and Sue both enjoyed hunting rabbits and pheasants out on the farm in November. It was so special for them to enjoy this recreation with their dad. We had many a delicious meal from the results of their hunt. Of course, there were always stories to tell about the skillful use of their guns and where they came upon their target. Jay has a few special memories of hunting for deer in the mountains with Elmer too, through the years.

Many funny things happened during the years the children were growing up. To review a few brings me a chuckle all over again. Twelve year old Linda decided to bake a chocolate cake while I went to the grocery store one day. She chose a Black Joe cake recipe. This called for a cup of black coffee. Upon my return, she announced to me that the coffee made the batter very stiff, so she added water. I thought a little and said, "What kind of coffee did you use?" I was appalled to learn she used a cup of instant coffee granules. We were eager to know how it would taste. Actually it did not taste so unusual, so we each had a big piece for supper. That night no one was sleeping at 2 o'clock. The girls said, "We can't sleep." On giving the dilemma some consideration, we realized the coffee was keeping us all awake. There was enough coffee in that cake to make 48 cups of coffee.

One evening our family went to prayer meeting. Sue said she needed to stay home to do homework. She said she would wash the supper dishes. When we returned, all the dishes were still to be washed. They were stacked up so neatly. She had an assignment for an art class, so she decided to draw a picture of all the dirty dishes stacked to be washed.

Esther was about 7 or 8 years old when Norma Jean was dating Larry. She was not quite ready for her date one evening when Larry was in the living room. Esther was chatting with Larry and upon noticing his large shoes, she asked him, "What size shoes do you wear?" He answered, "Size 12." "Wow, Norma Jean thinks hers are big and she wears size 9," said Esther.

Jay rode with me to town one day. He was about 6 years old. He said, "Did you see that tractor in the field?" "No, I didn't." Then he saw a couple other things I didn't see. He looked at me so amazed. "You don't notice anything," he stated.

Vera had a little friend, Lynn Duffy, who came to play with her after school. When Christmastime came she wanted to give her a Bible for Christmas. The children also wanted a Christmas tree. In my way of thinking there was only money for the tree or else the Bible. I'm not certain if it was the whole consensus, but at least Vera decided the Bible for Lynn was more important than the tree. I was so blessed to see these two girls playing in the play house under the front stairway, both having their own dolls and their Bibles.

When Vera and I would drive past certain houses on the way to Millersville, she would sometimes say, "Do those people know about Jesus?" It would put me to shame to think that I really didn't know.

Norma Jean would occasionally go to Gretchen's after school. One day she said, "I'm glad my daddy doesn't talk so cross like Gretchen's daddy does. I like my daddy better than hers." Yes, I thanked God over and over for my dear husband. He was a man of wisdom. I found God's order was the plan for me. I noticed I needed to give Elmer time to come to a conclusion concerning decisions that needed to be made. I was inclined to make hasty decisions and leave no time for the "head" to be in charge. God blessed me with a submissive heart that waited for God's best in many instances. I looked up to my husband with thanksgiving.

There is a classic example of "out of the mouths of babes" that came from one of our grandchildren. Rachel Stahl lived in our home for a short while. She and her brother were raised in Germany. One day her brother came to visit Rachel in our home. Our five-year old granddaughter, Amy, was also visiting us. We were sitting at the dinner table and Rachel and her brother were talking in German with each other. Amy could not understand a word they were saying. After a while she looked at Rachel and said, "Don't you know you should not talk with your mouth full?"

Another memorable one was when Matt was about four or five; he sat down to our dinner table and looked at our food. He pointed to one dish and said, "Yuk! I don't like that." I said, "Matt, we don't say 'yuk' at our table. We just say, 'no thank you' when it is passed." The next time he was at our table, he looked over the food and soon pointed to a dish he didn't care for. "No thank you for that," he deliberately said.

Another grandchild, Timothy, was at our table one day. I served cornstarch pudding for dessert. It had formed a skin over the top as it cooled. Tim paused as he ate it and said, "Grandma, I think you put a little too much cob in the cornstarch pudding."

The girls and I were sorting unused clothing upstairs one day. We came to a new red dress that I bought, but which the girls either did not like or it did not fit. "I think I'll give this to relief," I decided. "Relief? What's that?" one asked. "Why that's when you give something we don't need to a place where they pass it on to the needy people," I answered. "Oh," said Linda. "Then that is relief for them and relief for us!"

Teaching as life flows on about us takes place in subtle ways. Raising a family is a school for parents as well as the children. Things are caught more than taught. Be careful how you live it.

Our seven children have gone in different directions both geographically and in their work. Norma Jean taught school for several years before her children were born, and then served in her church and in her community as a volunteer. Sue taught school, and then devoted herself to preparing others to serve the Lord through Roca Blanca Mission Base in Mexico. Jay made a career of driving truck, with more than five million miles under his belt by now. Nancy worked in health care and then as a mediator. Linda did office work until her family of eight children came. When Linda finished high school she decided to go to Europe with a group, and used money we gave her for that trip. She chose not to go to college. Esther worked as a nurse, then as a teacher before her children were born. And Vera worked as a social worker in senior living and in hospice until her children were born. Many of these occupations touched the lives of individuals. We leave the results to the Lord.

We are grateful that our ministers at Millersville Mennonite Church, Herbert Fisher and Abram Charles, helped bring changes to the church that made it possible for our children to serve in various ways. In their teen years, our children taught Bible school and Sunday school at a mission church in York and at Millersville. The girls taught Vacation Bible School in many other places, including Wheelerville, Reading, Palo Alto and more. It was an adventure for them to go away for two weeks, and they had fun with the team of young girls who served the Lord in that way. Jay traveled with a group of men to Louisiana to help a Mennonite Disaster Service team clean up after Hurricane Betsy. Youth group activities and summer camp, Sewing Circle, and youth conferences all laid a good foundation for the ways they are serving the Lord today.

As parents we saw each of our children growing in their love for God. As we saw them struggling with decisions, we committed them to Him. There was no greater joy than to know they were happy in the choices they made.

Photo credit Jonathan Charles

1994—celebrating our 50th wedding anniversary

L-R: Linda, Norma Jean, Vera, Ruth, Elmer, Jay, Sue, Nancy, Esther

Many, but not all, of the greats and grands came to celebrate our 65th anniversary in summer of 2009.

The big move from Charlestown Road to
Manor Boulevard. April, 1973

CHAPTER TWENTY-FIVE

Exodus From The Farm

Elmer and I enjoyed seeing our children gain new work skills and new social skills. They brought many friends home after school or from church on Sunday afternoons. We had children at our table from York where the older girls taught Sunday school at a mission church. We had children from the "Fresh-Air" program, who came from the big cities for two weeks each summer. We invited men and women to our home who were traveling with choirs or other groups, and needed meals and lodging for a day or a week at a time. Our children became acquainted with the different nationalities and cultures these children and adults represented. We visited Elmer's mother in her home and at the nursing home after she suffered a severe stroke at age 69. There the children learned to appreciate and sympathize with the elderly.

As our family grew up they began knowing other young people their ages. Norma Jean went to the Lampeter Fair one autumn with a girl friend. A fine young man who was nearly 16 years of age was attracted to her. It wasn't long until their friendship turned into weekly dates. Our family loved Larry

Neff, too and a few years later they both went to Eastern Mennonite College, in Harrisonburg, VA. They attended college there two years and then got married on July 10, 1965. They made plans to move to Ann Arbor, Michigan, where they attended two more years of college. They both graduated from Eastern Michigan University the spring of 1968.

Norma Jean and Larry Neff were married in 1965.

Now our summer vacations started to take on new meaning. Michigan was 600 miles away. At the same time, Sue was in college at Morgantown, WV. We went to visit both of them one summer. Later Larry and Norma Jean moved to Indianapolis, IN. That is where we went to see their first baby, Stacy Jo, in September 1972.

In the meantime, Jay became well acquainted with the Weaver family that lived on a nearby farm we were renting from Armstrong. He liked doing the chicken and field work around their home. We had sold our farm to Armstrong World Industries in 1960 and we were now renting our farm, along with the farm where the Weavers lived. Jay and Fay Weaver were in the same high school class at Penn Manor. In their senior year Jay spent numerous evenings in their home and learned to enjoy their family and especially spent a lot of time with Fay.

One can hardly imagine the difficulty Jay had one day in announcing the shocking news to Daddy and me that Fay was pregnant with Jay's child and expecting a baby the following May. It was a heartbreaking fact and we needed wisdom and spiritual strength to know how to deal with this situation. We talked with Paul Ehrhart, the guidance counselor of the school, concerning Jay's situation. He said, "Mr. and Mrs. Rohrer, one can't go back, so we need to accept the circumstances and go on from here." How true. Jay loved Fay and

Fay Weaver and Jay were married in 1966.

they decided to get married at Christmastime in Fay's home church. They became established in their home in Manor Twp. Baby Rebecca was born shortly before Jay's high school graduation. She was our first grandchild, born in May 1967. Oh, how we loved her. We loved her parents also and God blessed us all with a forgiving heart. Being grandparents became an exciting adventure.

Fifteen months later, in August 1968, there was a second baby born to Jay and Fay. Her name was Amy. A year later there was a baby brother, Matthew, with which to share their mother's time and energy. These three children gave our family many new fun times and opportunities to entertain lively, little children again. After a busy afternoon I made the comment to Elmer, "Aren't you glad we have our grandchildren while we are still young?" He looked at me and seriously said, "You sound like you think this is all the grandchildren we will have!" We were so thrilled when Becky knew us as Grandpa and Grandma. We liked being grandparents.

Jay had trouble with allergies when he was around the cattle and the chickens. Therefore he could not continue farming and started doing long distance truck driving. Sometimes he was gone two weeks at a time. His trucking company was based in Omaha, NE. Jay realized he could spend more time with his family if they would all move out to Nebraska. This was another enormous decision for this family of five who had no relatives or friends so far from home. But the decision was finally made, and the summer of 1974, Jay's tractor trailer truck was loaded with their household belongings and they moved west. This was another exodus of a part of the Rohrer family from the homeland.

Some major moves were made a few years before this time. Nancy graduated from Lancaster Mennonite High School and received her training as a registered nurse at Lankenau

School of Nursing, in Philadelphia, PA. She was in love with her high school sweetheart, Clair Sauder, during those years.

On August 12, 1972 they were married. At that time Clair was serving a term of Voluntary Service in Alabama. He wanted Nancy to join him to finish the last year in Montgomery, AL. So this exodus took our dear Nancy to the south. Our next vacation trip drew us to places we never saw before in Alabama. We had some news to share with them the winter of 1973.

Nancy married Clair Sauder in 1972.

There was a new house being built just south of the border of our farm. Jay and Fay needed to move from the little house they occupied at Sporting Hill, near Manheim, PA. So after some serious thought and much prayer, we decided to buy the new house and move off the farm. Jay and Fay were pleased to move their family to the old farm house. They spent just over a year there before they moved to Nebraska. On April 19, 1973, we moved into the Bowling Green development, less than a half mile away, on the south border of our farm.

In the midst of planning our exodus to the new house at 1270 Manor Blvd., our Linda, who was dating her sweetheart, Elmer Landis, announced their plans to be married on June 16, 1973. These seemed to be the busiest years of my life. I did a lot of sewing in those days. Having made many dresses

Linda and Elmer Landis were married in 1973.

for our six girls while they were small, and lots of school dresses and skirts, I now was busy helping the girls make their wedding dresses and their bridesmaids' dresses. There were many decisions to be made about details for the new house. I made drapes for some of the windows.

Esther and Vera were in Lancaster Mennonite High School at this time. In August, 1973, Elmer and Linda accepted the invitation from Eastern Mennonite Board of Missions to go to Honduras as missionary school teacher and office worker at the Los Pinares Elementary School in Tegucigalpa, the capital city. This was another exodus from the home area. Their first baby, Christina, was born in Honduras in June, 1976, before their 3 years of service was over in July of that year.

In the meantime, Nancy and Clair finished their term of service in Alabama and made a move to Lexington, Kentucky, where Clair went to college and Nancy worked as an RN in the hospital. During this time their first baby, Timothy, was born in May, 1977.

Having graduated from Goshen College in Indiana, Sue became a happy physical education teacher at Lancaster Mennonite High School. The call came to Sue from the Eastern Mennonite Board of Missions to go to Honduras to teach in the same school where Elmer and Linda were serving. In 1975, Elmer and I took a five-week trip to Honduras over Christmas and New Year to visit our dear ones who lived in the mountains seven miles outside the city of Tegucigalpa. Elmer also helped in the clean-up work following a severe hurricane in San Pedro Sula. This was our first overseas cultural shock. We visited the town of Trujillo, where my sister, Jean, had served as a missionary nurse for eight years.

While Sue was in Honduras, she met a Christian man from Kansas, whom she desired to learn to know more intimately. Surely God was planning a most unusual relationship for them, and as their own story would prove, He brought them together for marriage on March 25, 1979. They moved to Kansas and finally followed God's leading to southern Mexico in 1991, where they founded a Bible school for leadership

Sue married
Duane Kershner
in 1979.

training. Nancy and Linda and their spouses returned to the Lancaster area to raise their families.

Our two youngest daughters, Esther and Vera, were making decisions about their schooling, their voluntary service and their careers during the 1980's. They had decided to continue their education at several different places. Esther became a Licensed Practical nurse and later graduated from Millersville University with a Special Education major. She worked at Friendship Community in 1980 and then as a teacher at Locust Grove Mennonite School, near Lancaster. Later, she returned to work at Friendship Community, a residential program for adults with developmental disabilities. While working there the first time, she met a fine young man, Marlin Myers. They enjoyed a few dates together before he moved back to his homeland in Florida. Ten years later he stopped for a visit at Friendship and who should answer the door bell but his old girl friend, Esther Rohrer. They renewed

their friendship and nine months later, on June 29, 1991, they were married on our lawn at Manor Blvd. Esther made her exodus from the homeland to Tallahassee, Florida.

Esther and Marlin Myers were married in 1991.

We now had a place to vacation in the winter of 1992 in the South. This started our yearly visit to Florida . We would visit Marlin and Esther on the way down and then go on to Sarasota, where we spent a few weeks during the cold weeks of winter up north. This went on for a few years until in 1995 we finally purchased a mobile home in Bahia Vista Estates, along with Harry and Evelyn Rohrer from Mountville, PA. We spent as many as three months in Florida each winter, and would get to see Esther and Marlin and their two children, at least two times each winter. Jeremiah was born in May 1992 and Jewel was born in September 1994.

Vera spent a number of years in Virginia getting her college degree in Social Work at Eastern Mennonite University. She found employment in Harrisonburg and was happy with her church and friendships. She decided to go to Temple University in Philadelphia, to get her Master's degree in social work. While doing her practicum internship in Chestnut Hill Rehab Center, she met a very special young man named William Foronda. His parents were from the Philippines, and he had lived in the Philadelphia area since he was four years old. Vera was attracted to Bill and Bill started to attend the West

Philadelphia Mennonite Church with her. Their friendship grew and they both were happy to be living in Philadelphia. They got married on May 29, 1993, and bought a house together. Alyssa was born December, 1994 and Andrew was born August, 1996. Vera's exodus was rather far from home also.

Vera and Bill Foronda were married in 1993.

Elmer and I missed our dear ones when they moved away from home. We always thanked God for the happiness they experienced being in God's will, wherever God called them. There were other grandchildren born during these years. Julie, July 1975, and Jimmy, August 1977, were born into the Neff family. Michael was born November 1979, into the Sauder family. The Landis family had Eric, May 1978; Jesse, January 1981; Gregory, April 1984; Peter, November,1986; Deborah, December 1988; Rachel, May, 1991 and Joseph, July 1993.

These grandchildren were all born within 30 years, scattered in ages, so that we had new grandbabies to love and enjoy all through those 30 years. There was again another thrill when our great grandchildren were born. Our first great-grandchild was born in 1987, and in April, 2015 we celebrated the arrival of great-grand number 27.

This exodus review is not complete until a painful part of our experience is recorded. After Jay and Fay and their three children moved to Nebraska, the cord snapped that held them together. The tragedy was heart breaking to all of our family. Jay moved out of the area. The story of their divorce is one that only Jay and Fay could give. God worked in their lives and each became a new person through those painful years.

God's grace is sufficient as we cast our burdens on the Lord. Elmer said, "We must give this to the Lord." We admitted our guilt and failures in what we realized could have been our mistakes along the way. We committed Jay and his family to the Lord and trusted Him to take us through the wilderness that seemed so dense to us at the time. We felt God's forgiveness, and our burdens were lifted at Calvary. We are still feeling the love between us all, including Fay and the children, which God has put there. It is such sweet peace, the gift of God's love.

After a few years Jay met Jane Eudy from Texas, whom he learned to love. They committed themselves to each other in marriage on October 22, 1988. She joined Jay in the trucking business and Jane helped to drive the semi millions of miles in the following years. They are very happy together. We are thankful for another dear member added to our family. Jane has two sons who are married. Jane is the grandmother of our six step-great-grandchildren.

Jane Eudy and Jay were married in 1988.

Fay and the children still live in Nebraska. Jay and Jane lived in western Montana, among the scenic mountains and wildlife of God's creation for a while, and then moved to Jane's home state of Texas.

CHAPTER TWENTY-SIX

Other Transitions

Now we go back to the early 1960's to that farm that we sold to Armstrong, but never moved away from. After the first three years were up and the last installment was paid, they offered a year-by-year agreement that could be canceled with a six month notice. These years brought changes. Broilers were being contracted, demanding larger broiler houses to be built for 30,000 to 50,000 birds. By 1959 we switched to all laying hens. We were feeding one hundred or more steers. Our dairy cows were moved to the Lebanon farm. Some additional acres of Armstrong land became available as some of the other neighbors moved away. We were now farming over 200 acres of corn. To plant, we used a six-row no-till planter, traveling five miles per hour, dropping 24,000 kernels per acre. Weeds were controlled by spraying chemicals on the ground. I remember receiving an award one year for a yield of 165 bushels of corn per acre on a test plot.

In the year 2015, Cliff Charles farms that land, using a 12-row planter equipped with a GPS monitor, planting 35,000 kernels per acre. Yields of corn are 225 bushels and more per acre. Corn is sprayed by GPS-guided tractors. All the operator needs to do is turn the tractor in the direction of the other end of the field, and then he can read a book if he wants to, until he gets there!

Many operations advanced in our time, from loading loose hay by hand, to loading loose hay with a pull-behind loader, to a self-tie baler, to a bale thrower loading the wagons. Wheat yields have risen from 30 bushels to 100 bushels per acre in my life span. The self-propelled combines came on the scene in the late 1940s. My dad started with a Massey Harris 7-foot clipper self-propelled combine. Now a thirty-foot header is used to harvest wheat. A 12-row corn head is used to harvest corn.

Production from Holstein dairy cows has increased greatly since our herd dispersal on September 8, 1978. That herd of 125 cows had a rolling herd average of 15,046 pounds of milk and 565 pounds of fat for the year. Today's records show some Dairy Herd Improvement Association (DHIA) rolling herd averages of 28,000 pounds to 30,000 pounds of milk with 900 to over 1,000 pounds of butter fat in a 305-day lactation, with three-times-per-day milking.

The corner cupboard I made for Ruth pictured in our dining room on Manor Blvd and where it is now, in Jim Neff's home.

Elmer-crafted furniture in our living room on Manor Blvd.

I made a step stool for each of the grandchildren. Jeremiah and Jewel Myers are holding theirs.

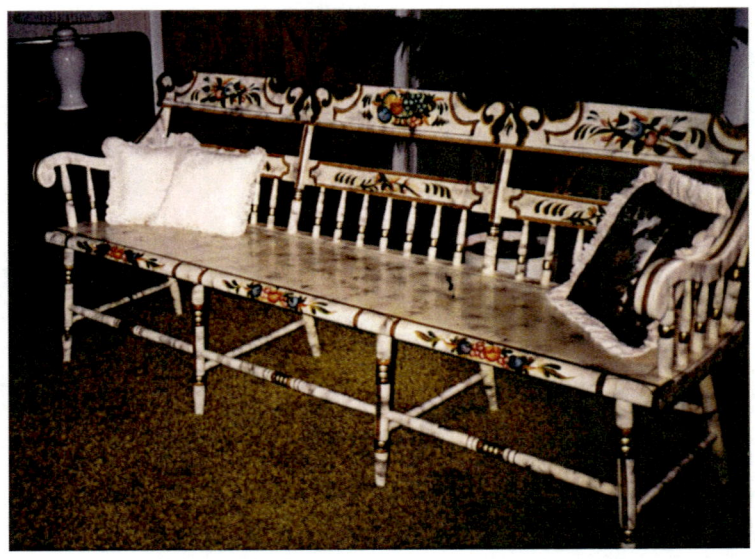

This is a replica of a 1850 angel wing design settee,
hand painted with smoked markings in the finish.

In my wood shop.

One factor in the increasing herd yields was genetic improvement through the use of artificial insemination. Prior to the late 1940s, each dairy farm had its own bull for breeding the cows. In the late 1940s we started using artificial insemination for our herd. With this new technology, a proven bull could be used to service innumerable cows. The dairy farmer could selectively improve his herd through choosing characteristics such as body type and milk production.

By 1970 we had closed out the poultry operation. 1973 brought another change for us. We moved off the farm to a neighboring development. We continued feeding steers until 1978 and closed out grain cropping in 1987.

I was 67 years old and looking forward to picking up on an interest in woodworking that I had in my younger years. In 1980 I had the privilege to cut down a number of wild cherry trees on the Armstrong property. I took the logs to a saw mill and stacked the lumber to air dry it. Some of these trees measured over 30 inches across the stump and I ended up with 6- or 7-thousand board feet of good cherry lumber, plus a good supply of walnut wood.

I saw potential in an old tobacco shed on a neighboring Armstrong farm that could be modified and take on a new name, "Elmer's Shop." Old buildings were a liability to Armstrong, so their answer to my request was, "Take it down and you can have it." That answer did two things. It gave me a 28x48 foot, 1½ story shop and also preserved an old method of mortise and tenon building. This shop was equipped well enough to take a piece of rough lumber and turn it into a variety of antique reproductions. I enjoyed the challenge.

Linda and Debbie load Debbie's chest. I enjoyed learning to make the dovetail joints on the chests.

Some trophies from my hunting days, including the black bear, which became a rug in our family room.

CHAPTER TWENTY-SEVEN

Hobbies And Hunting

Early in life I heard the quote, "All work and no play makes Jack a dull boy." I took it seriously. Having enjoyed rabbit and pheasant hunting and already being in my mid thirty's, I joined my brothers-in-law, Henry Leaman and Jay Garber, on a first day deer hunt in Juniata County. This was enjoyed for a number of years, but I was not contributing to the meat larder. The next move was to Sullivan County to hunt with my good friend, Ivan Gochnauer, Pastor of the Wheelerville Mennonite Church. It was here that I filled several tags for buck and turkeys, and in 1982 I tagged a nice black bear. I enjoyed two hunting trips to Colorado and was fortunate enough to come home with a bull elk and a mule deer.

Even hunting was changing. Much of the hunting land in Sullivan County was being posted and I was invited to buy into a camp in Lycoming County. As Ruth and I discussed this idea, we realized it was a privilege we were hoping for. We became part of a ten-member hunting group of fine Christian couples. The property included several hundred acres of hunting land, where the deer, bear and turkeys roam. It soon became apparent that we needed to enlarge the cabin and we made it large enough to accommodate families and Sunday school classes. What a blessing that has proven to be. We built a shuffleboard court as an outdoor game as well. By this time in our journey Ruth and I were both teaching Sunday school classes our own age and younger. These groups spent a couple days with us at William's Manor Retreat each year over an eighteen-year period.

I enjoyed the challenge of hunting turkey in the spring and fall, and deer each fall. I enjoyed being outdoors and seeing the game in their natural habitat. Bagging some game to take home to the freezer was a bonus. I provided a turkey for Thanksgiving dinner some years, and often provided venison for the freezer. The camaraderie of camp life established valued friendships and fun. I wrapped up my hunting years in 2009, when I was 89 years old.

It was in these years that I was elected to serve on the Black Rock Retreat board near Quarryville. I was also asked to serve as chairman of the benefit sale committee for this organization. Those eight years proved to be both challenging and rewarding. In 1990 we wanted to encourage people to donate antique items to the auction. We had a copper kettle in our cellar, and as I prepared it to donate to the Black Rock auction, this bit of verse came to my mind. Prior to the sale, I read this poem at the Black Rock Association meeting:

Must be 50 years since you've been hot,
That is, as a seething pot,
For to remember when you were used, I cannot.

I've been told by those gone before that you've made apple butter in days of yore.

Now-a-days that is bought at Bomberger's Store.

You look so black I cannot recall

Ever seeing you look shiny at all.

"No wonder," you say, "for many years I sat in that dark cellar corner covered over with this and that."

I confess I owe you a cleaning. In eight hours flat, I think you'll be gleaming.

So, here comes the vinegar and plenty of salt.

If I rub too hard, it's all my fault.

What's this I see? Dovetail seams! And here are some initials.

One wish I will make, that I could your maker's hand shake.

I need to tell you, you will be sold.

There is Black Rock Camp that we need to uphold.

You may move far or near,

But if you don't bring a pretty penny

I'll buy you back so you don't need to move any.

What will I do, you seem to beckon, in this new era you've come to reckon?

You will be in a lovely spot by the fireplace, good and hot.

Family photos you may hold, or the wood that once they put beneath you,

Now is placed within you.

A seething pot you are not,

But a copper kettle is your lot.

I was happy to buy the kettle back, because I wanted to give it to our son-in-law, Larry Neff. The kettle was at one time owned by Larry's grandparents.

We took a lot of venison off the mountain at William's Manor Retreat.

A picture of camp life at William's Manor

Monday is the first day of buck season, and the anticipation is gaining momentum day by day. Some hunters have already arrived on Saturday to do some scouting. Sunday morning may find some of us at the Methodist church nearby in Oriole, for what they call a "quickie service" planned specially for the hunters. Others of us traveled to camp on Sunday afternoon.

Supper is over. The roster is signed. Rifles are all sighted in. Some of the guys gather around the stove to tell stories that we've all heard before, hoping for new stories to tell from this year's hunt. A couple guys are deeply engrossed in a game of Othello, and still others are playing Crokinole. After a while the Captain announces, "Breakfast at 4:00!"

There might be a quick review of the channel setting on the walkie talkies and the names we used as a handle. We all used handles to preserve some privacy, because anyone on the mountain could tune in to a walkie talkie conversation. We had Candy Man (John Groff), Candy Man Jr. (Marvin Groff), Carp (Amie Warfel – he's a carpenter), Tomato Man (Cliff Charles), Welder (Mahlon Shenk), Chipmunk (Alvin Weaver – just because there are chipmunks there), Hay Man (Abe Lefever), Beef (Paul Shenk), Magnum (Don Hoover), and Dry Cleaner (Lloyd Heisey). I was called Ranger, and that calls for an explanation. One day as I approached my tree stand, I noticed an orange glow about five feet above the roof. They told me it was the "Ranger Station," hence I received my second nickname, "Ranger Rohrer." To this day, no one will admit to putting that orange ball up there. I think if they could have found a current bush, they would have used a light bulb instead.

Time brings changes. Those mountain climbs proved to be a big challenge as the years went by. We sold our share of the camp in 2010, when I was 90 years old, but we do maintain a visitor status. It pleased us when our granddaughter, Stacy said, "Grandpa, I would like my children to have a cabin experience like I had." So a visit was planned in 2014 and the children found their way to the top of the mountain. They climbed those fifteen steps to the top of my tree stand and showed me a picture to prove it. We had a great weekend as thirty of us ate, played and prayed together. Those times spent at William's Manor Retreat were special, not only in the game that was tagged, but also the relationships amongst us, and the community contacts made precious memories.

Meals are highlights at the cabin, with the hunters and with the family.

Heading towards retirement

By this time the farm work was reduced to growing only corn, which meant there was more time for community involvement, as well as time to spend in the wood shop. Some time prior to this I was introduced to pitching quoits in boxes ofsoft clay. These quoits stayed where one dropped them.

This surely surpassed my experience at the family gatherings where we would hammer two stakes into the ground, twenty-one feet apart and hope to have that quoit stay where it dropped in the dirt. I was intrigued and challenged and I soon became involved in some serious quoit pitching competition. Monday evenings I could expect a number of men to gather at our shop and enjoy some challenging games. Yes, we even tallied the number of ringers each one pitched. My partner, Jay Kauffman, and I won a fair share of the games we played. I do remember on one occasion I put two ringers on the peg, only to have them topped by two more by my opponent. Now that's competition.

As we gained some sons-in-law in the family I was challenged to the game of golf and at sixty-six years of age I bought my first set of golf clubs. Some years later, Ruth joined me in this venture. Yes, we enjoyed our time together with other friends. Ruth developed a nice smooth swing. We justified this sport by playing on the lower priced courses and playing in benefit games for Landis Homes, Black Rock and others.

It was through these years that I found a challenge in the wood shop, trying to duplicate various antique items, such as dovetailed corners on blanket chests for the grandchildren. I had started to make a gun cabinet for Jay when I was challenged by a mini stroke (TIA). I struggled with balance and my thinking was slow. Jay said, "Dad, forget the gun cabinet," but I said, "No, Jay, I need the challenge." And so it was that with time and courage the cabinet was brought to completion. It took extra time to figure out the settings on the saw, and how to do the next step. But the challenge kept me going. "Thank you, Lord." The other thing that kept me going was the fact that turkey season was approaching. Doctor Kemrer said I could go, so come November, I went hunting again.

In the early nineties we started our yearly treks to Tallahassee, Florida, to visit our daughter, Esther and family. We also went to Sarasota and Bahia Vista Mobile Home Park. It was there, on those beaded shuffleboard courts, the game of shuffleboard took on a new interest for us. The Crokinole board game also gave us a challenge when I started reproducing them. The first one that was sold at the Sarasota Christian School sale sold for ninety-five dollars. The last one that we offered in year 2010 was auctioned off at seven-hundred dollars plus a five-hundred dollar matching fund offer. We soon found other benefit auctions that we support with these games. Other Crokinole game boards that we sell privately help support the Victory Latin American Outreach Mission at Roca Blanca, in Oaxaca, Mexico. This is where our daughter, Sue and her husband, Duane Kershner are serving. At the last count the total game boards I made stands at one hundred seventy-seven. It's fun to know that lots of families and groups of friends have happy times when playing this game.

CHAPTER TWENTY-EIGHT

A Lesson Found In Wood

It's a piece of wood, but what do you see? Let me draw your attention to the drawer fronts on the walnut secretary desk I made for Ruth for our 50th wedding anniversary. The wood fibers are interwoven in such a way that they become very strong and hard. This is where a limb has grown out from the trunk. That limb attachment to the trunk is strong enough that it can bear the weight of fruit and thus complete the growth cycle.

The graining on those drawer fronts is a thing of beauty. The beauty reflects the symbolism found in John 15 about the vine and the branches. Again in Ephesians 5:22—6:4, which describes the importance of the bonding and love relationship between Christ and the Church, husband and wife, and parent and child relationship, all bonded in love.

Yes, God is credentialed above all others. Bless His Holy Name. Ruth and I are very comfortable with this pattern. I must admit that there are times Ruth waits for me to take the lead. Ruth says she feels more comfortable when I take the lead.

I made mention of a fruit-bearing branch. Yes, we have added to the family tree six daughters and one son. Each one with their own uniquely chosen spouse have blessed our family and also added 20 grandchildren plus 24 greats and still counting. To you this account may be a list of numbers, but to us it is a list of blessings. I say with III John 4: "I have no greater joy than to hear my children (and grand children) are walking in the truth." It is for these that we pray almost daily.

Ruth at the desk I made for her, seated in our living room at Landis Homes.

Crokinole boards have provided a lot of friendly competition with family and friends. I made 177 game boards and donated them to benefit auctions or, from the boards I sold directly to people, I gave the money to Roca Blanca Missions in Mexico.

L-R: Bill Foronda, Andrew Foronda, Vera Foronda, Elmer Landis, Ruth, Elmer, Joe Landis and Peter Landis.

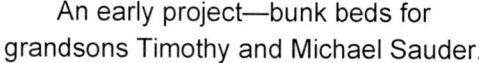

An early project—bunk beds for
grandsons Timothy and Michael Sauder.

Edith Herr provided essential help when Nancy and Linda were small. We included her in our family until her death in 2012.

CHAPTER TWENTY-NINE

Our "Extended" Family

Our children remember setting the table for meals in our farm kitchen. Invariably they would ask, "How many will be here this time?" That question came because the family was always coming and going. It also reflected the reality that we shared our table with lots of other people. Yes, there was always room for one more. We had neighbor boys who came to help with harvest, and stayed to enjoy strawberry shortcake at our table. We hosted children from the Fresh Air Fund for many years while our children were growing up, beginning when Norma Jean was one year old. One Sunday I was called to the phone at church. A grandmother from our congregation had been sent to the hospital, and they needed someone to keep her infant grandson for a while. He stayed with us for six months.

Several years we hosted International students who needed a home for a week or two over Christmas, which gave us a taste of many cultures beyond our own. We also hosted Doni, from Pakistan, and Janet, from Jamaica, while they attended Lancaster Mennonite High School, and Karen, Pat, Mary Kathryn and others, who attended Millersville University.

Our children enjoyed overnight visits from their cousins and their friends, and if there were people who needed lodging while on tour with a choir, etc. we often welcomed them to our home. Later, several of our grandchildren stayed with us for weeks or months while they attended school, or worked in special assignments in our area. Yes, if there was an empty bed in the house, we were usually willing to offer it to someone who needed a place to sleep.

It is understandable that our young children were sometimes a bit resentful about sharing our time and attention with so many other people. We hosted lots of people from many places, and now, in retrospect, our children tell us that the practice provided a wider world view for them than if we had just kept to ourselves. We find it interesting to note that our adult children often demonstrate this same kind of hospitality in their own homes.

Edith Herr had a special relationship with our family. Edith was my friend at church when we were in our upper teen years. She lived with the folks she worked for on a farm nearby. Edith was the one who went with Elmer and me on our first date. Later, she spent her days off from work in Lancaster with me on the farm. The children were little and I needed help. Edith could care for the family for a day when Elmer and I took a day off now and then. She helped me with garden work, and with canning and freezing food for the winter. Edith always needed my encouragement and we shared days together all through the years. We included Edith in our family gatherings and holidays for many years. The Lord blessed me with strength to visit her weekly when she was in a nursing home in her later years, and I was blessed to be at her side when she passed on to glory at age 92.

I also had a special friendship with Rita Bleacher. Rita became a frequent part of our family activities after Esther got married in 1991. Rita lived at Friendship Community when Esther worked there, and she deeply missed Esther when she moved to Florida. Rita started to come to our home one weekend each month, and joined us at church, helped at the Re-Uzit Shop in Columbia, and attended family gatherings with us. Rita often tells me, "I love you very much as a friend." The structure of our time together has changed, now that we live at Landis Homes. Rita attends a day program here at Landis Homes, so we still have lunch together occasionally in the dining room.

A winter view from our apartment at Landis Homes.

CHAPTER THIRTY

God's Faithfulness

This is the middle of 2011. I love being here!

But where am I? I am at a different place than I was when I wrote my life story in year 2000-2002. I am older in years and 88 years old is not what I expected. I am able to walk, think, see, hear and share with others. Who are the "others?"

The "others" are God's special favor to me. First is my dear husband, Elmer. We have shared 67 ½ years of marriage, walking together up hills and down. Last evening we walked to the wood shop at Landis Homes Retirement Community, near Lititz, PA. It is not far from our apartment. The sky was so lovely, with white puffy clouds above us and only the blue sky between us and heaven. Or so it seemed.

We moved here in October, 2010. Elmer turned 90 years old

in March that year and then said, "Now it is time we downsize to smaller living quarters." That was the signal for us to pass the word to the family. It started a whole string of events.

Our daughter Nancy picked up the idea and off we went with her in the month of May to Landis Homes to speak with Donna Shank regarding an appropriate residence for us. The cottages there seemed desirable, but they were all either occupied or spoken for. Donna had some other ideas or suggestions to offer us. There was a new phase of building in progress. We saw the new buildings called "hybrids." In my words, this means a cottage within an apartment building. We were impressed with the idea of having plenty of room with windows bringing in lots of light and a balcony instead of some lawn outside the door.

Along with Nancy we pondered the idea and chose a lovely spot on the 3rd level, which is the top floor, having the eastern exposure. From there we could look out over the fields and ponds with the promise of many lovely sunrises to admire. The garage and storage area are on the ground floor.

The work was only beginning. The family responded with excitement and a strong willingness to help. A sale date was set for October 15. That started the action. The basement, the loft above the garage, the closets, the shop and every spot above and between needed sorting.

Our new apartment was in the race as well, only to be finished 2 weeks after the sale date. We had a PODS sitting in our driveway for things to go with us to 1533 Wisteria Drive at Landis Homes. Sale items were gathered. Some items were given away and some put on the junk pile.

The most outstanding blessing for the sale day was that all seven of our children arrived on the scene from so many different locations. Norma Jean and Larry came from Indiana. Sue came without her husband, Duane, from Mexico. Jay and Jane arrived from Texas. Nancy and Clair and Linda and Elmer contin-  ued supporting us from their nearby homes, Esther and Marlin drove up from Florida and Vera and Bill from Philadelphia. Thanks to our loving heavenly Father for His guidance and answers to prayers for this momentous day.

The day of the sale arrived and Mr. Kline said his team would take responsibility for the action. The time to sell the property came at noon and it was finally sold to a dear couple,

Shawn and Amy Smith. They were so pleased to have the two acres, with the house and shop for their use.

Elmer's shop things and the lumber were dispersed to the pleased bidders. The household things were bought by our family members, neighbors, friends and others from farther away. We had given a sum of money to each of our children to use to purchase items at this sale, if they so desired. I made up my mind to not fret at some of the low prices and unknown locations of my prized possessions. God helped us feel satisfied and happy that all that work was now behind us.

By October 28, 2010 we were into our new abode and were realizing we were blessed to be enjoying this experience as a reasonably healthy and very happy couple. "Thank you, God!

The "hybrid" apartment building where we live at Landis Homes.

CHAPTER THIRTY-ONE

A Scattered Family in 2015

When I consider the last twelve years since I wrote my life story there are significant changes in our precious family. I am now 92 years of age and Elmer is 95. We are both driving the car and able to care for ourselves. This is an amazing blessing. We treasure memories of our 70th wedding anniversary celebration in February, 2014. We now number 72 in our family, scattered across the United States to Mexico and the Canary Islands, in many different towns, cities and states. My computer helps us to keep in touch via emails. We also send birthday cards with personal messages to our seven children, 20 grandchildren and the greats. God knows about us all and we pray regularly for each one by name.

Our grandson, Tim Sauder and his wife Frances bought a small farm near Quarryville, PA, which adds a farmer to the mix again. It looks like our great-grandson Theo Rohrer, Matt's son, might be a farmer some day. At age 15, Theo enjoys working with his Grandpa Majerus on his farm in Nebraska. There are no other farmers among the businesses of the family since Elmer retired from farming in 1987. We sold the Manor Township farm in 1960 to Armstrong World Industries. We had two farms in Lebanon County and sold them in 1991.

Our grandson, Jeremiah Myers, has developed an interest in woodworking and carpentry. Currently he is taking classes and working in this trade, and has even made a Crokinole board patterned partly after the boards his grandpa makes.

We enjoyed driving to Sarasota, Florida for 18 years in the winter time. We enjoyed being a part of William's Manor hunting camp in Lycoming County for 27 years. The family gathered there at intervals and many memories were made with the children and grandchildren at that mountain retreat.

As our girls turned 60 years of age we ladies celebrated at various places. We met at a time-share in Nashville, TN for a few days to celebrate Norma Jean's milestone of 60 years. Jay's wife, Jane, also met with us. Elmer and I, along with our girls and some of their husbands gathered at Roca Blanca when Sue turned 60. Nancy and Linda planned their joint celebration as we met in Savannah, Georgia. These were delightful times and we look forward to sharing with Esther and

Vera in the near future.

We kept in touch with Esther and Marlin's family when we were in Florida. We had a visit with Sue and Duane seven different times at the mission at Roca Blanca in southern Mexico. We visited Larry and Norma Jean in Indiana numerous times as well as their daughter Julie in Iowa. We are privileged to visit Vera and Bill and various grandchildren in Philadelphia. We traveled to Iowa, Indiana and Nebraska to see grandchildren, and to Texas to visit Jay and Jane after they moved to Decatur in northern Texas.

Elmer has lost sight in his left eye since we moved to Landis Homes, as a result of the accident he had many years ago while baling hay, so we do not drive such distances any longer. We have made several visits to these dear ones more recently by flying instead of driving. We are happy and comfortable here at Landis Homes, and appreciate the deep love that our family shows for us.

As Elmer and I combine our life stories we realize the faithfulness of God has prevailed. There have been many joys; some shades of sorrow contrast the high spots. May God receive all the glory in this story of "Our Journey Together" from 1920 to 2015.

CHAPTER THIRTY-TWO

Travel Journals

Our Trip to Niagara Falls 1959

Anticipation—Wednesday, August 5

This is Linda's seventh birthday, which was only part of the main event of the day. The rest was the fun of getting everything together in the dining room to pack for our camping trip to Canada and New York State. Excitement was running high at that point. Esther said, "Only one more sleep, then we will be going." Ten year old Jay wishes we could take Tippy, our pup, along. All are wondering if we can get everything in or on the `57 Chevy station wagon, including all nine of us, ranging in age from 3 to 14 years of age plus Mom and Pop. "There is always room on the top" is our only hope of taking everything.

Thursday, August 6

Had a hearty breakfast and left home on Thursday at noon-time. After finishing a huge job of packing food, clothing and shelter—enough for about eight days, we started out but didn't go more than a few hundred yards till we heard a patter, patter on the roof, reminding us of our amateur job of putting the canvas on top of our luggage. We headed for Elizabethtown after we stopped to adjust the canvas. We had a light lunch near Amity Hall, enjoying the peaches Grandma Garber sent along. We saw the pretty Susquehanna River and noticed "Jay's Restaurant" at Liverpool. We saw "Ruthie's Truck Stop" near a lovely gladiola field above Liverpool.

We decided to stop at Ivan Gochnauer's farm at Wheelerville where Bible school was in progress. We arrived at Ivan's at 5:15 and they invited us to Bible study in the evening. Also they agreed for us to put our tent in their hay field for the night. This was an ideal spot for our first experience of camping outdoors.

Elmer and the children got to work on the tent which was pitched for the first time without too much trouble. We made supper of spaghetti and fried eggs which everyone thought tasted much better than at home. By 7:45 we were on our way to church. Elmer had the devotions and Ivan spoke on the third commandment. We came home to our tent where we all eagerly found our nests in our cozy sleeping bags. We had just enough room for all nine of us with two cots under the tarp between the tent and the rear end of the station wagon. Elmer and I slept in the car on an air mattress.

Friday, August 7

We woke up at 7 o'clock with beautiful sunlight casting its beams in all the "peep-holes." It had been a cold night but everyone managed to keep warm. We heard remarks like these: "I slept good;" "Vera Ann was as snug as a bug in a rug;" "Split level sleeping;" "My feet were cold, so I pulled them up to my bottom." Each one was proving to be a good camper. Daddy was the first to wash his face in the dew. Breakfast was enjoyed by all. By 11 o'clock we were packed again and on our way to Watkins Glen. We had a light lunch before going through the Glen.

What a long and beautiful trail! We followed the Indian Trail and the Gorge Trail. The little ones climbed, jumped, ran and walked. They were all good sports but I was glad they were no younger. We loved the tunnels, walking under the falls, the whirlpool holes, the bridges and even the 700 steps or more. Every corner had a surprise for us. But most of all we were glad to see the Chevy again when we got down, with its can of fresh water for us thirsty pilgrims. We enjoyed the trail and the falls so much and left there at 4:15. We saw some large vineyards around Seneca Lake, which is one of the Finger Lakes.

Next we found where Ed Meixell lived. Ed had been a feed salesman on our farm. He came home around 7 PM and was surprised and pleased to see us. He and his wife informed us of some camp sites. We went to Robert H. Treman State Park to set up our camp with a group of other campers. It was about dark, so we hurried and made supper, which tasted soooo good---yellow beans, red beet eggs, juice, etc. Daddy and his helpers put up our home which went faster than the first time and by 10:30 we were all snug in bed. The evening was much warmer than it was at Ivan's. Vera Ann had a slight fever this evening so we gave her some aspirin which quickly made her feel better.

Blowing up air mattresses took about all the wind we had left. "Whoever blows one up can sleep on it." Even I blew mine up between puffs.

Saturday, August 8

"Rise and shine" calls Daddy at 7:30, as the rest were slowly waking up. Each slept especially well. It was rather warm but all were quite comfortable and in ship-shape that morning. Each one ate breakfast and helped break up camp. We saw a pretty little water falls back of our camp site. We spoke with some neighbors. Our large family and complete luggage set-up seemed to fascinate folks. Five year old Esther got to play-ing with some children and was reluctant to leave. We left camp at 10:45 after rounding everyone up, including Esther who we found at the camp warden's office with her new friends.

Next we headed for the New York Turnpike, traveling up along one of the Finger Lakes, named Cayuga. We ate some lunch at a rest stop on the Thruway. We took the Niagara Thruway across Grand Island. We went over two high bridges, saw a large steam boat, and stopped to get our first view of Niagara Falls. It surely was a mass of water coming down over that falls. The younger ones soon got tired of that stop and we had quite a few miles to Kitchener, so we stayed in Niagara only a short time, hoping to see more of it when we returned. We had so many parking fees and bridge tolls to pay that it made Esther and Vera Ann think we were giving free will offerings. When we were ready to go over the bridge to Canada they wanted to give the man a penny too.

After customs we got on the Queen Elizabeth Way to Hamilton. We saw lots of vineyards and fruit orchards. Saw some views of Lake Ontario. The sea breezes were real refreshing on this hot day. There were a few white caps on the edges of the lake. We crossed Lake Ontario at Hamilton and saw some large boats to the excitement of the children. Such high bridges!

Next we were headed for Sidney Roth's near Shakespeare. This was a long drive through Canada. The small children got a little tired and I was beginning to wonder how everyone was going to get washed up and rested to be fit for Sunday. Esther heard we were going to someone's home and said, "Aren't we going at a picnic and stay all night?" We stopped for ice in Kitchener and then went on toward the Roth's, not knowing where to find them as yet. They were friends of my sister Jean, who was a friend of their daughter, Irene. They did nursing together in Honduras. On the way from Kitchener to Shakespeare we saw signs to "Brunk Revivals." So we decided to look them up. Arrived there about 8:30, so we used the rest rooms and stayed in the car. We heard George Brunk preach a little and as we inquired where Sidney Roths live we found they were not far away. In Shakespeare we bought groceries and then phoned Roth's but no one answered. While we were there someone knocked at our window and asked if we were looking for Sidney Roths. To our great surprise, it was their son, Howard, who was coming home from the hospital where their second son was born that day. He said his folks were looking for us and that we should follow him to get there. The Lord certainly answered our prayer for guidance. We found a note for us on their garage door saying we should make ourselves at home. So we took a little supper in and ate it. Then we started to bathe the younger ones who were surely dirty.

Then the Roths came home and insisted we use their beds, of which she had plenty. We all cleaned up and crawled in good, clean, soft beds, thanking the Roths and the good Lord for all these kind comforts. The family all loved the nice rooms each one had.

Sunday, August 9

We rose at 7:30 after a wonderful night of sleep. Had a delicious breakfast of cereal, juice, eggs and toast. I appreciated Sidney's prayer for devotions so much. We left for church about 9:45. We enjoyed the Sunday school hour and noticed the differences from our usual schedule at home. We met quite a few nice people who knew Aunt Jean. George Brunk preached. We each enjoyed our Sunday school teachers. We met Mrs. George Brunk.

We went to the Roth home for a delicious ham dinner. We all had a tremendous appetite. We will all remember the good little pickled corn ears that we ate for the first time at Roth's. After visiting a while we all had a good nap and then we went with the Roths to the tent meeting. George preached on Jeremiah. We wished we could be there on Monday night. We got several invitations to spend some days with Canadian folks. We went to the Roth's again for the night after a most enjoyable day and lots of good fellowship.

Monday, August 10

We arose at 8 o'clock. The barley harvest was in progress at this time and Sidney thrashed out a load of barley. It was quite interesting to see the various ways of harvesting it. The fields are so level and the roads are all straight and good. Some are stone roads. We ate a big breakfast again of oatmeal, juice and eggs. Elmer had devotions. We packed our suitcases once again. We thanked the folks for all the kind hospitality and hoped we can return it to them some day. We left the Roth's at 11 o'clock and headed for the Welland Canal and the Locks. We turned off the Queen Elizabeth Way just in time to see two large ships go through the locks. We saw the gates open and the water level going down. We enjoyed this very much. We also saw two other large ships go through the drawbridge.

We arrived at Niagara Falls about 3 PM. Someone asked us to sleep at their Tourist Home that night and he showed us where it was. We liked it for $12.00. Now we could see the lights on the falls at night time as well. We took a long walk on the Canadian side of the falls. It surely is a wonder on God's earth. The water was as clear as crystal. Next we went down 230 feet on an elevator to the rapids below the falls. We liked the big tunnel down there.

After this we made our supper and ate it at the Glen Park below the falls. Here the kids played up and down on a big hill. They saw and chased some chipmunks and climbed a long flight of stairs down to the rapids. It was all fun. About 9:15 we called home to Grandma Garber and found all was going well. It was good to hear her voice and she was glad we were enjoying ourselves. Next we saw the colored lights shining on Niagara at night. These were rather pastel shades and we enjoyed the beauty. After the lights we went to find the floral clock which we missed when we were down that way. We found it beyond the power plant. It was lit up and very beautiful. We heard it chime at 10:15. Then we went back to our apartment at Niagara. It was nice and quiet and clean and neat. We were all really tired after a wonderful day of sightseeing at Niagara Falls.

Tuesday, August 11

Everyone slept rather late that morning after a good night's rest. After our devotions we were on our way by 10:30. We took a good last look at Niagara Falls and went south along the beautiful Niagara River. We found a good spot to prepare and eat dinner along the river. Then we went toward Fort Erie and Buffalo. We saw large boats again and the big flour and cereal mills in Buffalo. We drove on part of the new skyway. Then we headed for Alleghany State Park. As we entered the State Park we saw a big turtle on the road for the first wild life. We drove on to the Quaker Area. We saw two groundhogs and then Jay saw the first deer. Next we all saw two deer and then a couple more. There were thrills for all. Linda said, "I'm glad you are only allowed to go 25 miles per hour. I think some black trees are a bear." Next we found the tenting ground was all occupied and one cabin was left. So we went to see it and decided to take it. Then cabin eight on Brow Trail was our home for two nights.

We unloaded some things and then went for a drive and a short hike. We came back and ate supper on the porch. After supper Esther said, "Ah, here is a little doggie at the steps." And to our surprise it was a big raccoon with his paws on the steps and his nose at the porch, begging for supper. We gave him some bread and he even ate some from Jay's and Sue's hands. This was all pretty exciting. After this we got ready for bed and our 7 cots and 2 air mattresses took up almost all the available floor space. We had a small electric refrigerator. The children placed bread around and on the porch to see if something would eat it over night. We were all tired and by 11 PM everyone was asleep.

Wednesday, August 12

We woke up about 8:30. The cabin got quite cool over night. Jay checked on the bait outside and found all was eaten but a bit on the screen door. The chipmunks were busy this morning, eating the bread around the cabin and even some from Susie's hands. It was lots of fun watching them stuff their little mouths full and then come back for more.   Jay and his daddy took a long hike up the mountain and spotted a black squirrel and a deer before breakfast. We did our morning work and then everyone ate a big breakfast and we had devotions.

By noon we were ready to swim and decided to call the food we ate our dinner also. It was a hot day so swimming was fine even if the water felt cool. First we tried the pools. We got two big balls and an air mattress for some fun. About 2:30 we decided to go to the lake about 9 miles on the other side of the mountain. Here the swimming was perfect. Each one had a lot of fun with the raft. The small ones enjoyed the sand. I rested awhile and then rode the raft boat while Esther and Vera Ann took turns pushing. In the meantime Elmer and the three older ones took an hour ride in two canoes. This was enjoyed very much although they found it took a good bit of energy to row so long.

About 7 PM we left for our little cabin on the other side of the mountain. There we made a good supper of noodles (to Esther's delight) and doggies and chips. We went to bed earlier this time. By 10:30 all were asleep on our good cots. The weather was really warm and the evening did not get very cool.

Thursday, August 13

We aroused everyone earlier this morning. By 7:30 we were up to the tune of the bluejays. We ate bacon and eggs for breakfast. Packed up everything again and said good-bye to Cabin # 8 on Brow Trail. But then we discovered we locked the keys inside the cabin. So we needed to get the master key and then return it.

We could see a lot of oil wells as we left the park going toward Bradford, Pa. We drove through the lovely mountains of northern PA. Around noon we stopped to see Alvin Millers at Ulysses. They have a small dairy farm. Their Bible school was in progress at York's Corners in the mornings. We also went to Freeman to visit Henry and Norma Breneman a few minutes. They have Bible school in a pretty little white church in the mountains. We were surprised to see my cousin Rodney Houser there as well. They were all from Willow Street, PA.

We ate our noon meal in the church yard at 4 PM. After finding my pocket book in the church we left there for the last long stretch home. We may reach home tonight yet or we may stop off somewhere to sleep first. At 7:45 we were around Lewisburg and had about 100 miles to go yet. After a short stop and rest we decided to go on home that evening and sleep in our good beds. We all seem to be as glad to get home again as we were to go last week. Even 10 year old Jay says, "I'll be glad to get to work again."

The mountains were beautiful as we came down through them to the New York line on Route 15. One range after the other entertained us with beauty. The little villages nestled like a picture scene among the many ranges. Our hearts turned merry as we hurried home at twilight. The children started singing and we sang "rounds" and choruses for an hour or more. We praised God for each other and all His many blessings that we enjoy. The nearer we were to home the higher the anticipation ran. The younger ones mentioned every hill and curve ahead of us, till finally we rounded the last corner and there we were on "our road." At 10:15 we were in the kitchen, home at last. How good it looked!

Jay hugged the pup, "Tippy." Some got a good fresh drink of water. The mail was piled on the table. There were cheers and much joy from all. Thank you, dear God, for such a lovely season of vacation and for the safe journey.

Quotes and words to remember from the 1959 camping trip to Canada:

Esther says "Is this today or tomorrow?"

"If they come to our house, they can have our bed," eleven year old Susie says.

"I hope we have the house redd up when they come," Norma Jean, who is 13, says.

"There is an Amish combine," Jay says when he sees a grain binder in operation.

At a detour and rough road, Vera Ann says, "Hey, why do them people do this?"

"My belly is soakin' hungry," five year old Esther says.

As we cross a creek, three year old Vera Ann says, "Hey,

swim!"

After the Aero ride, eight year old Nancy says, "Man, that was fun."

Seven year old Linda says "It wasn't even scary."

At supper time, Vera Ann says, "Come all people."

Almost home—"I can't wait till I see Tippy again—I hold her first," ten year old Jay says.

"I hold her second," Linda says.

"Maybe she has pups!" Linda says.

"Aren't they kind people!" Nancy says after leaving the Roths.

Rohrer Family Vacation
July 31 to August 8, 1962

1957 Chevy Station Wagon and a Pop-Up Camper

Monday, July 30 —the Day of preparation

"The girls can all help Mother today," Daddy said this morning. So prepare we did! We washed and ironed till everything was clean and neat. We also prepared a number of food dishes to take along. Jay mowed yard and cultivated the garden. Daddy got the car ready and did other errands. The biggest event of the day was when Daddy finally got home with the Porta-Camper trailer about 8:30 in the evening. He and Jay set it up and everyone was thrilled to get in and look around and inspect the drawers and cupboard space.

Verna and Musser Ebersole, our farm helpers, thought it was fine and roomy. They had thought perhaps Musser would need to come on behind us with the big blue truck and haul our "stuff," but now he changed his mind. Everyone went to bed really tired, too tired to pack as we had hoped to do. But tomorrow may be another day.

Tuesday, July 31

It was a little hazy in the atmosphere as the family pulled away from the farm about 10:30 am. This was not as early as we wanted to be on the road when we got up at 5 o'clock this morning. Everything had been placed in the dining room the day before that was to go along with us in our Porta-Camper. But it always takes a while to pack as many things as our family might need for 9 days of vacation.

Everyone was a little impatient to get going. So after filling every drawer and cupboard and ice box in the trailer we closed it up with room to spare. This was contrary to what most people thought would happen, because folks in general wondered where we would be putting everything for so many people. All 9 of us from age 6 to 17 years, plus Mother, 39, and Daddy, 42, were filled to the brim with anticipation, so thankful that the Lord had made it possible for us to take this vacation, as Daddy expressed in devotions this morning.

As we pulled away and went toward Columbia we found that the trailer seemed to make us jerk along a bit and made our speed a little slower than we are accustomed to. But even so, we feel this is a wonderful way for 9 of us to travel. It is a comfortable day as we turn south on Route 111 for Washington D.C. about 11 o'clock. The children enjoyed seeing a helicopter on the ground at York. The Rice Krispy candy tasted good while going down the highway.

Daddy asked Mother to drive as we went toward Baltimore. This was surely some modern road system around Baltimore and became a little complicated as we wanted to turn off for Washington D.C. so Daddy took the wheel again. We only got a peek at Baltimore. The children had a high time getting the truck drivers to blow their air horns. The sandwiches we brought along tasted good as we drove along. We noticed lots of pretty bridges as we passed under the many underpasses.

We entered Washington about 1:30 and had trouble finding certain streets. We decided to find a camp site before we visited the Institute. Saw a fire boat shooting water really high. Saw big airplanes, water boats, bridges and more bridges. The weather is hot now! We hunted and hunted for a parking space and found there was no room for us to camp. Finally we found room in a parking lot. Aren't we lucky! Got some water out of our jug to drink and started walking. We walked about six blocks to the Smithsonian Institute because we especially wanted to see the Space Capsule that is like the one John Glenn used to go around the world three times. Well we saw it and looked inside and decided he surely was in a squashed position.

We only saw a few parts of the Institute because the children grew quite tired and it was soon time for it to close. We walked back to the car and enjoyed the rest of our good cold water. We left Washington via the bridges and route 50. About 5:30 we stopped in Fairfax, VA for ice cream cones and filled the jug with lemonade. How refreshing! We went through the Civil War battlegrounds of Manassas, Battle of Groveton and Battle of Bull Run. Virginia looks beautiful. The meadows are green, in contrast to the dry pastures in PA.

We found a secluded spot just south of Culpeper that would be ideal for our camper. We went to someone who could tell us if we could camp there. The neighbor let us call Hoffman Implement Service and the man said, "Go ahead." The lady gave us some water. We came back to the clearing on top of the knob and Mr. and Mrs. Hoffman were there to meet us. What a wonderful camping ground. They looked inside and thought the tent was neat after we set it up in a hurry. Vera Ann, Norma Jean, Nancy, Daddy and Sue slept outside on mattresses or sleeping bags. We asked Mr. Hoffman what we could pay him. He said, "You can't pay for this kind of spot." How true!

We got our chicken corn soup heated up and had a lovely supper with tomatoes and lettuce, cheese and crackers. Yummy! We sang "Praise God from whom all blessings flow." Twilight is a wonderful time to eat and did we have fun! We could hardly wait 'til dishes were washed to get to bed. Beds were provided in the trailer and outside. Then each picked where to sleep. Upset the fruit basket was the order for everyone and each ended at a different spot than where they began, except Sue, who ordered the new sleeping bag long already and got it to use. We all laughed so much till we even got aching sides and tears and coughing spells. "No wonder those slumber parties get out of hand," we said. Vera Ann couldn't go to sleep so Norma Jean told a Bible story and started singing songs until she was off to sleep. The katydids

Rise and Shine the first morning of the trip, near Culpepper, VA

were loud so I suggested they count the songs the insects sang. Every time someone moved the whole trailer moved and so we were soon all rocked or sung to sleep! Thank you God for the lovely night and place to be.

Wednesday, August 1

Mother awoke before the first bird was singing. Soon they started taking turns serenading us. And did they sing, mockingbirds, bluejays, cardinals, bobwhites et al. Esther was awake next, closing her zipper to the window beside her top bunk. It looked like Norma Jean and Vera used their mattresses for pillows, because they slid off their mattresses and practically under the trailer during the night. Daddy peeked open to see the last stars disappear but fell asleep again.

But by 6:45 all were awake and saying how wonderful we slept. Linda said she got "all shook up..." Yes, we could feel every body's turns. Nancy said she was a little cool, but mostly we were all cozy.

Soon the bacon was frying and 1 1/2 doz. scrambled eggs were made. Lemonade and Wheaties were also enjoyed. The dishes were washed, teeth brushed, faces washed, beds made, floor swept, clothes put away, devotions and then we were ready to close up again. Reluctantly we said good-bye to that beautiful spot and pulled off about 9 o'clock.

Next we needed some ice which we found on our way to Charlottesville. Road #29 was good and the scenery pretty. Esther, Linda and Vera had a neat bed in the back of the station wagon. Saw the pillared houses around Charlottesville and went west toward the Blue Ridge Parkway. We were hardly around the first curve of the Parkway when we saw a doe and two spotted fawns standing in a row across the highway, looking straight at us. They turned and hurriedly leaped back across the grass and into the forest. Such "Oh's and ah's" you seldom heard. Excitement plus!

It is getting cool and a little too hazy to appreciate the lookout views completely high in the mountain. We saw a big bare spot across the way and Jay said, "I know, that's just one of Paul Bunyan's footsteps." Then Jay saw another deer. We went on and on through and around and over the mountains. Elevation at this high point was 3590 feet and the scenery was great.

At Roanoke we left the Parkway and took Route 221 which was parallel with the parkway but in the valley hills instead for more speed. At the southern border of Virginia we stopped for gas and got the idea to hunt the Stoltzfus residence just inside North Carolina at Jefferson. We had seen them in PA and perhaps we can sleep around there. We got into NC about 6:45. There were lots of little farms all over the big round hills. We tried to find Aquilla Stoltzfus, stopping at so many different places till someone finally knew of them.

Seeing the steep hills with cows grazing on the sides we wonder how the cows ever lie down. We think perhaps they roll down the hill and have already churned butter. After about 500 turns around the hills and asking about six times we finally found Aquilla Stoltzfus' home in the middle of the mountains at a neat little place. It was 8:45 and to our surprise someone was home. Lydia Kurtz was keeping house and welcomed us gladly to do whatever we please.

So we set up housekeeping and ate a quick supper of red beet eggs, peaches and cereal with milk, and sugar cookies. It tasted wonderful, especially at this late hour. We were soon ready for bed. Daddy, Mother, Esther, Vera and Nancy in the tent and Jay and Sue in bags on the lawn. Norma Jean and Linda were in the station wagon. Norma took flash pictures of each bunch and we were soon in dreamland with only God and the pup, Cutie, keeping watch over us.

Thursday, August 2

Mother didn't get awake till 6:30. Soon Daddy and the rest in the trailer were moving around too. We had a nice cool night to sleep and all were comfortable. The dog, Cutie, was ready to greet us at the door and he did not miss a thing we did this morning. Esther even invited him in the trailer a bit to look around. He was just a little brown rat terrier and he surely was cute. We all enjoyed a good bath in the house. Our breakfast consisted of what our supper had been planned had it not been so late. So we enjoyed spaghetti and peaches with cereal for some. Never thought spaghetti would taste so good in the morning.

After cleaning everything up and visiting with Lydia a little we finally pulled out at 10:30. Such hills and mountains we had never seen before. They are high in altitude around here and raise a little corn and some tobacco. We see lots of horses. We wish we could have seen the Stoltzfus family but we are especially glad Lydia was there. We left a couple notes and a little gift of money. We took a picture and said good-bye. We stopped across the way at the Big Laurel Mennonite church and had devotions. Norma Jean led and thanked God for the blessings we enjoyed, asked His blessing on the Stoltzfus family and asked for His guidance and protection for the day.

After we were on the winding road again and going through

the beautiful scenery the girls started singing rounds. They were really pretty and funny at times. It starts to rain as we look at Grandfather Mountain. At Linville we took the Parkway and the clouds and fog hide the scenery below. There were tunnels along the way and the fog cleared about 1:30 when the scenery became gorgeous again around Mount Mitchell. Craggy Pinnacle was all covered with rhododendron. The wild flowers are so pretty. Yellow, white, purple, orange and red with black eyed Susans all along the way. There was a long descent to Asheville as the little ones started singing "Praise Ye the Lord, Hallelujah." Stopped for gas and food at Asheville and took Route 19 to Cherokee. On the way we came to "Ghost Town Chair Lift." We decided to take the chairs. It took lots of courage for Mother to do this, but she decided to go since everyone wanted to go so badly. It rained while we went up with 2 in a seat and each chair using an umbrella that we brought along. Sue sat alone. Mother was sure glad she could sit with Daddy and she watched the umbrella more than the scenery. After going way up to the top of the mountain we took a bus ride around Ghost Town and could walk through the old stores and shops, a bank and hotel and an old church. To go back down the children (all but Esther) went down on the chairs and they just loved it. They liked the scenery but Mother wanted to go down on the cable car instead. So Daddy and Esther went along with her. Seems Mother likes her feet on the ground.

In Cherokee we looked for a campground. We got groceries and also found the state parks were filled and we were told of a family campground on Route 19 where we got the last space for trailers. We were so glad to get it and soon got set up— just in time, as it soon began pouring rain. We all crowded into the trailer and were dry and thankful. We made supper of doggies, baked beans, tomatoes, bananas, red beet eggs and some cupcakes from home. Everyone needed to sleep and eat under shelter this night on account of the heavy rain. So Norma Jean, Esther and Vera slept in the station wagon. Daddy and Mother slept on the floor of the trailer with their feet in the drawer space after we put the drawers on top of the stove and refrigerator. Jay, Linda, Sue and Nancy were in the bunks. What a neat and compact arrangement and to all a good-night!

Friday, August 3

It rained a lot during the night but the canvas house kept us dry. Had our usual hearty breakfast after which Sue led our devotions. We were all packed up by 9:10 and drove through Cherokee again. Saw fancy Indians and lots of shops. Took Rt. 441 and stopped at the Oconaluftee Indian Village. This was the most interesting and educational feature of our trip, so far. We saw how the Indians made many of their crafts and utensils. We hiked through their nature trail and saw quite a few hummingbirds and many garden plants growing.

It was gorgeous!

About 11:30 we started to cross the Smoky Mountains. We went to Clingman's Dome and walked the half mile trail up to the observation tower which is 6,699 feet above sea level. We enjoyed going up the high ramp to the tower. We could see the old, rugged, wind-and-snow-beaten balsam trees which were beautiful. The fog and clouds were blowing around and once in a while the sun would take a peep at us. There were only a few glimpses of the other mountains below. We went down again to our car and back to Rt. 441. The views of the

high mountains were great as we drove down through the other side of Tennessee. We kept looking for bears but failed to see any, except Norma Jean thought she saw one. We turned into a park along a stream to find a camp site for the night. We found Elkmont Campgrounds and picked a nice secluded spot for us near the rushing stream. We unhitched the camper, and then we all were off to see the Tuckaleechee Caverns.

They were amazing to all of us—especially the kids were simply thrilled with the long passageways and formations. It was only opened in 1954 and it is fascinating to hear how it was discovered.

We got gas and groceries and went back to our little trailer. Set up our housekeeping and got our hot dog and tomato supper ready. We ate it at a table by the light of the lantern. Our bedtime found Norma Jean and Esther in the car, Jay, Nancy and Sue in sleeping bags on the ground and the rest in the tent. This is really a nice place to be.

Saturday, August 4

What an exciting night! During the night, around 3 o'clock or so, Linda got a little cool so Daddy tucked her in a bit and then after hearing the lovely sound of the mountain stream he came to the rear end of the trailer to talk to Mother a bit about the swell location and some other nice things. He never thought of the fact that the trailer was unhitched from the car and would be easier to tilt. He sat on the edge of Mother's bed and BOOM! CLANG, CLANG!! We see-sawed back and hit bottom! We were horrified, but soon realized what happened. Mother said "What shall we do?" Daddy said "Guess we'll need to pull it back down again." "Shall I help?" asked Mother. "OK" said Daddy. So he stepped up toward the front and Mother followed. Soon Ker-plunk and we were back again! Then Daddy stayed in his bed.

The clanging noise was the porch supports falling down on the stones. Linda was in the bunk above Daddy. She was hanging on to her bed for dear life, not having any idea what had happened. Daddy and Mother just laughed so badly that they could hardly stop. Finally they all went back to sleep again.

Jay was the first to awaken this morning. He looked around and then put up the porch supports. He came in and said "Hey, did you see anything of that big fellow last night?" His eyes were big and he looked excited. We said "Did you hear what happened?" "Yes, I heard it. Do you think it was a bear?" We laughed as he said how scared he was when it all happened. He just stayed flat so the bear would not get him too. Well he soon got it out of us about what really happened and soon all were told about our crazy fun! Did we laugh for awhile!!

We ate breakfast at the table—cereal, sliced peaches and Nancy's biscuit rolls made over the fire. Daddy led in devotions. We were a little slow to leave that lovely spot. It was about 10:30 till we left.

We stopped for some metal screws to tighten the trailer frame before we started off to Knoxville on this warm and sunny day. Everyone was eagerly looking forward to visiting our long time friends, John and Ruth Schock who live at Sparta, Tennessee. Elmer and John were high school friends and Elmer was best man at their wedding. Now they are the pastor couple at the Sparta Brethren in Christ Church. Norma Jean studied some Spanish on the way and we sang some songs and watched the scenery go by. The Cumberland range lies between Knoxville and Sparta. "So here we go, on the plateau on top of the mountains" and crossed "Daddy's Creek" and a few miles after that was "Ruth's Grocery." The singing isn't going very well along here. No one can agree on a pitch for "Let us sing together our joyous song." How crazy.

We stopped at Crossville on the plateau for some lunch. Wondering what to do with our trash from the car... the fellow told us to just throw it out on the curb. Near Sparta we saw a sign "DeRossette." Decided to stop and phone to find out where the Schock's live, but immediately saw a sign "DeRossette Brethren in Christ Church" up on the hill. A cheer went up from all. We drove up to the church and a white house was beside it with a mail box for the mission in front. We parked and out came Ruth, all full of smiles with a hearty welcome for each one by name.

John was at the radio station. Ruth showed us where to park the trailer behind the church in the grove. Such a lovely place to call home! Our youngest ones saw the swings first. Ruth said John would be glad they like the swings. Soon we met "Shaggy," the large black and white Persian tom cat. He was so cute! We asked Ruth if we could use her washing machine and soon washed sheets, towels, pj's and some underwear and wash cloths. What a privilege. Each one took a bath which felt so good. John and Elmer started out where they left off the other time with their usual jokes and tricks. Ruth soon had a delicious supper of potato soup, tomatoes and peach pie.

After supper we got ready for the Southern Singing at the church. Everyone that could sing really made a joyful noise as they all sang with energy. Jay said he could hardly keep a straight face and Esther held her ears shut at first (the singing sounded so different from what they were accustomed to). Then they started asking little girls and other individuals to sing. Next they asked the Rohrer family to sing. Esther and Vera tried singing "Jesus Loves Me." But half way through they got "tickled" (as the southerners called it) and had to laugh. So we all tried to sing "My Jesus I Love Thee." Everyone did their best in the congregation and we all enjoyed the evening a lot.

Back at the house we had Kool-Aid, popcorn and cookies. Archie Fikes from Nappanee, Indiana arrived with their daughter, Erma Jean, who is 17 years old. Soon we were all tired enough to go to bed. Norma Jean slept in the house with Erma. Jay was in Johnny's room. Johnny is the Schock's only child and is around Norma Jean's age. Sue was in the sleeping bag and Daddy, Mother, Esther and Vera were in the trailer. The end of a wonderful day had come. It was 10 o'clock their time but 12 o'clock our time. No wonder we were all dead tired!

Sunday, August 5

"Happy Birthday" to Linda today. Now she is 10 years old. Norma Jean and Erma learned to know each other well enough to talk till 3 o'clock in the morning. It felt good to sleep late this morning. We went to the church services. Archie read the Bible and Elmer had prayer. Elmer also taught the youth class. There were around 125 people present, with a good variety in ages. They sang Happy Birthday to Linda in Sunday school. John preached on the text from Revelations 16.

Ruth had a big dinner for us in the basement of their home, consisting of meat loaf, baked potatoes and macaroni, beans, cole slaw, jello and a birthday cake for Linda. In the afternoon the young folks took a drive and the older ones were lazy and visiting went good on a hot afternoon. Supper consisted of sandwiches and watermelon which we ate out in the grove. Elmer called Musser, our helper at home, and he said all is going well except the auger belt tore. They had some rain.

Services were held in the evening at the church again attended by quite a few people. Elmer read devotions and had prayer. John interviewed Archie about his work as a printer at

Nappanee Publishing House in Indiana. Norma Jean read a poem, Esther and Vera so sweetly sang "My Bible and I," Erma played her accordion, Sue and Nancy sang "How Great Thou Art." Connie, one of the local girls, played her accordion too. John preached about having Christ in our boat as we go over the sea of life.

After church we enjoyed talking to some of the members. Three more girls arrived from PA to visit John's for a couple days. The Fikes are leaving early in the morning for Florida. So we said good-bye to some nice, new friends before going to bed.

Monday, August 6

We had breakfast about 9 o'clock. We cleaned up the tent and trailer. Ruth and Mother had a talking session. Daddy got the car greased while John went to a ministerial meeting. After a quick lunch 15 of us went to "Clifty" to go swimming. Six rode in the station wagon and the rest went in John's little trailer behind our car. This place was about 8 miles back a stone road to a creek that was rather low due to low rainfall. The stream had a solid rock bottom and a big hole where we could swim and have fun. The water was the warmest we ever swam in and we had such a lot of fun! We found a small pair of boy's overalls to play tag with. Everyone got all wet except Ruth Schock's head. Johnny could not go along because he had to work at the grocery store. We missed him. He has quite a little business in electronics started on his own in his bedroom. He is 18 years old and has lots of radio, stereo, recording and amplifying equipment to use and rent out to others. We returned about 5:30 at 10 miles per hour, so that the ones in the trailer would not get so dusty.

Ruth soon had hamburgers ready to fry over John's charcoal fire in the garage. We enjoyed the watermelon after Johnny came home from work in the heavy rainstorm. We played ping pong and shuffleboard till we were really tired. Vera Ann said, "This was the biggest and best day." This was our last night at Schockie's.

Tuesday, August 7

Mother and Daddy got up early to start packing at 5:30, Central Standard Time. The children got up about 7 o'clock and we had everything in the trailer about 7:30 when suddenly the sky got really black around us. Jay and Daddy hurried to get things in place and quickly put the trailer down just as it started pouring. We got the top snapped shut while the trees did their best to protect us a bit, but all three were quite wet when the last snap was closed. We finally went in to the house with umbrellas and then had a jolly breakfast time with some more of Ruth's good buttermilk biscuits. After the ping-pong table was cleared in the basement we played "Blow the ping-pong ball" with the Rohrers against the rest of the bunch. The Rohrers are the windiest because we won 11-7.

We finally gave our good-byes with everyone wishing we could stay longer. John wanted Esther to stay and she would have been willing it seemed. Johnny wished he had a brother like Jay. Jay loved Shaggy a little longer and Daddy finally went out in the rain to get the car a bit closer. He could hardly get it started. He thought the motor was too wet. Finally it started, but it did not hit up very well. John looked under the hood and Daddy got out to investigate. To his surprise the spark plug wires were unhooked at places. Daddy knew who did that immediately. John said he just wanted to try one more way to keep us a little longer. This was the last joke for the pair. Elmer and John always were a pair! About 9:30 Central Time we pulled out through the rain. It was hard to leave as we all enjoyed the visit so much. Jay even had a few tears.

It stopped raining as we went over the Cumberland Plateau toward Knoxville. This was a hot day to drive home after we stopped for a few incidentals and set our time ahead two hours and headed toward Virginia on Route 11. Norma Jean drove about 100 miles, driving through the old battleground near Bristol. It was about 7:45 when we looked for a place to sleep in southern Virginia. Daddy was looking for some hills that were grazed and spied some near Roanoke. We drove back a small macadam road and then saw lights in a little white farm house off a stone road. We drove in their lane on the hill. The lady came out and Daddy told her what we wanted. She called her husband from a little chicken house on the hill. They were quite happy to let us set up our tent back of their house. Mr. and Mrs. Thompson were most accommodating. They gave us big light and 6 air mattresses plus 3 sleeping bags to use.

We got ready for bed in a jiffy. The children blew up the air mattresses and it seemed everyone wanted to sleep outdoors except Mother. So Nancy, Esther, Mother and Norma Jean, since she had not slept in the tent before, started sleeping in the trailer. After a while Vera Ann came in and woke Mother and said she wanted to sleep inside. So Mother woke up Norma Jean and finally she had ambition enough to trade with Vera. Then Mother sang awhile to Vera and we all went to sleep. We needed all our covers because the air was cool. How glad we were for such a good place to sleep. Thank you, God, for providing all our needs.

Note: These Thompsons are farming as a sideline. Mrs. Thompson works in a bank and Mr. Thompson works as a dealer for large equipment.

Wednesday, August 8

We all woke up to the tune of the Bob White quails. It was rather foggy and the dew was really heavy. All the sleeping bags were wet on top, but all slept well within them. We all got dressed in a hurry and then talked with the Thompsons and showed them inside the trailer. These fine people seemed really glad we stopped. They gave us a bag of delicious apples and some of their tomatoes to take along. We left at 8:15 and stopped for devotions. Mother led this time. In Roanoke we had a mechanic take care of the car while we all went to a nice restaurant for a good breakfast. The hot cakes and maple syrup servings were huge and delicious. Esther and Vera Ann had French fries and chocolate milk for breakfast because that is what they "really wanted." Jay thinks that breakfast will hold him over till we get home.

We left Roanoke at 10:30 and thoughts of home are coming fast. Esther thought this morning that we might not know where we live or which house is ours. "But when we see cute little Neal outside in the yard, then we will say 'Here is where we live'." Nancy thinks she would like to live in this little trailer all the time if there were not so many of us. At times the children have a little trouble agreeing on things and they argue once in awhile, but on the whole everything goes very well and they are all good travelers.

After being on the road for awhile again we heard some tin rolling off the side of the road. Jay said, "There goes our hubcap." We turned around and found it lying in the field. We put it in the car and were on our way toward Natural Bridge. Had a little ice cream at noontime and Norma Jean takes the wheel as we drive through the Shenandoah Valley toward West Virginia. Linda announces that she has at least 57 mosquito bites. Nancy has 64 on her arms, legs and face and Sue says, "Just be glad you don't have 80 some mosquito bites like I have." Esther has too many to count and Norma Jean didn't count hers. Sue and Nancy start the game of counting cows and burying them at the cemeteries on their sides of the road. We saw a thermometer that said 97 degrees which confirms it is a hot day.

We see signs such as "Sweet Sue's Beauty Salon," "Linda's Restaurant," "Jay's Department Store," and "Garber's Ice Cream." We see a movie advertized about "Esther and the King." We see a sign "Elmer Deer Road." We go across Harper's Ferry as we get into Maryland and cross the PA line about 4:30. Cheers go up for we are so eager to get home. Route 30 looks so good to us at York, and it is after 5 o'clock. Vera and Esther say they want to go over to Verna's as soon as they get home and say "Hi to Neal and Bevy." Things are starting to look familiar to everyone now.

As we got back to Rt. 83 near York, Jay said, "Now we went around the block, let's go again." But Daddy believes we better work awhile first. And we all agree, because we are about broke. Daddy thinks it is about time to hunt a place for the night. Norma Jean says she knows some folks near Millersville that might let us sleep on the other side of their house. There was some discussion as to which way to go when we got as far as Columbia. Norma Jean wanted to go via Mountville. She is thinking of her new friend, Larry Neff, who lives there. Daddy wanted to go by Washington Boro to see the crops. Daddy won and Norma said, "Perhaps Larry would not be home from work anyway yet at six o'clock."

The Charlestown road sign looked good at Washington Boro. Esther thinks we ought to "burp" the horn from now till we get home. Since we don't do that they "holler" instead. Then "Sing, sing together, merrily, merrily sing" is the tune. And Esther says "Praise the Lord, we are home soon." A big holler went up from all as we pulled into the parking space in front of our house. We hurriedly carried everything to the house so we could take the trailer back. Mother washed it inside and it really looked as good as when we got it about 10 days ago. How well it served us!

Everyone enjoyed these days so much. We all had experiences we shall never forget. Thank you, dear Lord, for bringing us safely home again!

Sayings and Quotes

Jay finds a feather flying around in the car as we start. He throws it out and says, "Look sonny, you are going to get lost," and throws it away.

Vera Ann says, after we were all packed up, "I hope this day will go fast, because I'm so anxious to sleep in here!"

After having gone about 50 miles Mother said, "Just think, we are off." (I felt relaxed already)

Nancy mentions that this is an "interstate' road as we entered Maryland.

"That little trailer follows us just like Mary's lamb."

Nancy is on the Blue Ridge Parkway and says "Even if I am a book worm, I can only read a couple words at a time. There's too much to see."

Linda, as we are almost at North Carolina, "We'll feel a bump when we get in it, won't we?"

Nancy in North Carolina, at a poor-looking little farm says, "Look, a cow in the front yard. Now isn't that awful?" Jay says, "That's their lawn mower, now don't make fun of it!"

"How would you like to check THAT fence, Daddy?" Sue said, as we gazed up at those terrific hills where the cattle were eating.

Vera Ann, thinking we might sleep at the Stoltzfus home, said, "Oh, must we sleep in a house?"

Passing out cookies in the car, Jay says, "You get finger service!"

A fellow was blowing his horn behind us while Daddy was parking our long vehicles and Jay says, "Just button your shirt, Buddy."

"Doesn't the air feel good? It is so soft," Norma Jean said, along the stream in the Smokies.

Vera Ann's concern among the Indians was, "Mother, do you think he (or she) knows about Jesus?" Also in a restaurant she wondered if the lady waitress from York, PA knew about Jesus.

About to cross the time line, Daddy says he wonders what it will feel like to slip back one hour. The rest wondered if we might feel the line or the bump.

When we were waiting for our curb service order we felt quite silly. Nancy says, "We will have to tell them we are from the sticks, but we are not hicks."

After leaving Schockies, Nancy says, "Aren't they nice people? About as nice as you can find anywhere."

Vera Ann was wondering where we were going to sleep the last night. Daddy turned in a dirt lane and she said, "Oh, Daddy, you drive me crazy."

Vera says, "I wish we could keep this trailer all the time."

Jay told Nancy the top bunk was hard. Nancy says, "Well, isn't that the crude way of livin'?"

Vera says "I wish we could keep this trailer one more day so we could play doll in it."

Esther says she does not like the last day of a trip, cause then the fun will be over.

Jay says, "I'll never forget last Saturday night when we were at the 'Singing' at Schockies. They sure put us to work." Ruth told us those people enjoyed hearing our accent as much as we enjoyed theirs.

Something didn't smell good when we were close to home. Nancy said, "Maybe the cat died."

Debbie and Peter's Adventure with Grandma 1993

It was springtime in 1993 when Elmer and I went to our hunting camp, called William's Manor Retreat. We took Peter and Debbie Landis along this time in our Chevy pickup truck. Peter was home-schooled so he was on a field trip this time. We stayed in the cabin over night and got up rather early that lovely morning in April.

Elmer took a hike in the hills to see what kind of wildlife might be in the field or in the shale pit. The rest of us ate breakfast and then decided to take a hike as well. I was a 70-year old grandma. Peter was seven years old and Debbie was five years of age. We started out by walking to the nearby reservoir where our water supply for the camp gathered. The lively stream that tumbled down the mountainside entered the reservoir there and then flowed down a waterfall on its way downstream. I had a walking stick or cane along with me.

The children soon started to hop and jump over the stream above the reservoir and Debbie excitedly said, "This is glorious! Aren't we having fun, Peter? Least I am!" We kept following the stream and their excitement rubbed off on me. I said, "Would you like to see where this stream comes out of the ground, away up in the mountain?" Yes, they agreed and we kept on jumping from side to side of the happy water falling over the rocks as it tumbled down the hill. We finally arrived at the spot where the spring began its journey from a space under the grassy area just ahead of us. We were all pleasingly fascinated to observe this phenomenon.

Now, should we turn around and go down to the cabin again, I pondered. I knew Elmer would be eating breakfast and then I expected he would drive the 7 or 8 miles up to his tree stand, because he wanted to see what the winter weather did to it and the area around his hunting spot. So I said to the children, "How would you like to see Grandpa's tree stand? We could climb on up the mountain and then drive down with Grandpa." Oh, yes they agreed to this idea.

Before long we saw a tree stand, but it was not Grandpa's. Each hunter had his own tree stand in different parts of the mountain. Elmer's was on up where the drive came in a couple miles from the main road. That is where he shot a couple of his nice deer in the past years. So we kept climbing on up and had to climb a little slower as we aimed to get to the top, to the narrow drive with its tracks that were made in the mud during the winter hunting days. Yes, we finally made it to that landmark.

Now we needed to go left, past the mud hole and then on till we saw the wooden steps up to the wooden platform where Elmer could watch for deer walking among the trees down below. But there was no sign of Grandpa's truck. No, he was not there yet. So we could turn around, and walk along the drive up there and perhaps we could meet him as he was coming in the drive there later on. This was easier walking since we were on a level driveway up on the top of the mountain and going away out toward the macadam road that we used when we drove to the cabin.

By this time it was 10 o'clock and we were thinking of taking off our sweaters and even having a drink of water. As we saw some spring flowers along the way, Peter would pick a few and Debbie would say, "When is Grandpa coming?" We would see a fallen log along the way and sit and rest a little. We saw the remains of a big pile of snow at one spot and even saw a deer cross the path far ahead of us. A spot came in sight where we could turn to the right and take a trail down the mountain. It looked like the trail on the border of our property. It could be the one Elmer would take groups down when they took hikes to the top of the mountain. So we could go down that path and get back to the cabin.

This suited all three of us. We moved along easily but soon the path ended. I told Peter to go down a little further and see if he could find where the trail started again. Debbie and I followed and at one place we sat down and slid part way before we could stop. I said, "Debbie, I think we must pray that God will help us get back." So we bowed our heads and I prayed "Dear God, we are having a difficult time and we need your help to know what to do. Please help us get to the cabin. Thank you, dear Jesus." I thought to myself, "What a poor grandma I am to take these dear little ones on such a difficult walk. Forgive me, dear God." We turned to look up and tried to get up the bank. Debbie got hold of a young tree and I said, "Pull yourself up." And she did. I did the same just as Peter came back on the scene. Debbie said, "Peter, we must pray!" "I already did," said Peter. He could not find a path. "Peter, you are the man. What do you think we should do?" A seven year old is young for such a question. "I think we should go back the way we came," he answered. "Well, let's try going on out this drive and maybe Grandpa will come up soon," I said.

So it was downhill after we got to the drive again and we started on our way. Yes, there was the paved road out ahead of us. We noticed the flash of a car going past the intersection. We took a few faster steps and soon we got to the blacktop of the main road that went on down the hill toward the Ravensburg State Park on our right. "We must walk on the left side," Peter said. The guardrail protected us from the drop down to the stream. A few cars came up the hill. I had my sweater tied to my waist and carried my cane. We watched for Grandpa's truck. Peter said, "What we need is a taxi, Grandma, or Grandpa's truck." "Yes, I'm praying for someone too, Peter, that can pick us up and drive us to the cabin." We saw a small building on the park property and yes, it was a restroom. But it was locked.

We walked on a little further and there was a big black automobile parked near the little lake on our right. A man was in the car and I suddenly thought perhaps he could drive us home. We went to the window and I said "Hello." He returned the greeting. "Sir, we took a long hike into the mountain this morning and now we are so far from the cabin that we need a ride. Would it be possible for you to drive us to our place a few miles from here?" "Why, yes," he answered. "I was fishing here in this pond and was not catching any fish, so I was just resting here a little while." "Well, we are pretty tired," I said. "Yes, I was watching you in my mirror and I thought you looked all tuckered out," he answered as he motioned for us to get in the back seat. "If you know how to get to your place, I will take you there."

It didn't take more convincing as I assured the man I knew the way and thanked him warmly. As we took our places in the big back seat I noticed a big sign tied to the seat where the driver was sitting in front of me. Printed on the sign in large letters it said, "MOM'S TAXI SERVICE 75 cents for the first mile and 25 cents for each additional mile." "Peter, look at what this sign says. "MOM'S TAXI SERVICE" "Sir, you are an answer to our prayer. We told God we needed a taxi and here you are! Oh, thank you so much!"

We drove into Rauchtown and turned right at the crossroads.

Then another mile and turned right again. We went on and there was our lane on our right. It wasn't long till we saw the cabin. The man said, "I agree, this would have been quite a trek for you."

We stopped near the door and I said he should wait a little till I get some money. I stood my cane by the door, but lo, it was locked. Elmer's truck was parked at the usual spot but no one was home. I knew where the extra key was back of the old pump trough and soon got it to open the door. I quickly got a piece of paper money out of Elmer's wallet. I noticed a note on the table that said, "I am going to the top to look for you." Oh, no, and now we are here. I went out to the man and he was putting a match to his cigarette and Peter was saying, "Don't you know you should not do that?" "Oh, yes, but..." as I handed him the money. He looked at it and said, "Oh, this is too much, I told you I didn't want anything." He handed back the 20 dollar bill, as he started his car to go on his way. I had not realized that it was a twenty that I pulled out of the wallet.

Peter and Debbie ran into the cabin and raced for the bathroom. Just then Elmer was on his way coming out of the woods and saw my cane by the door. "Oh, thank you, Lord. I believe they are home," he thought as he rejoiced in his heart. The next half hour included much reporting by both of us as I quickly put a pot of water on the stove to make macaroni and cheese for the hungry hikers. Elmer tried to explain his side of the story. He realized I possibly took the children for a hike in the mountain. Could we have gotten lost? He waited a long time, but we did not return. Yes, he had planned to drive up to his tree stand and do some trimming up there. But, oh, no. He would not do that if we were lost in the mountain. He may need to ask the neighbors to help search for us. So he would walk up along the stream and call for us and listen for the chatter and response. But finally he turned and came down again as it was time to eat.

Oh, yes, that macaroni cooked a little and I added cheese and put it in the dishes for each of us. Oh, it did not cook long enough. But Debbie and Peter ate it and actually never forgot how good rubbery macaroni tastes when one is so hungry.

But Elmer and I have never forgotten how happy we were to see each other after all that scenario and testing of our faith. Praise God for caring for his children, both young and old.

As I ponder this experience in 2015 and compare it with Ezekiel 43:1-12: I see God expressing His longing to reside among us. His glory is found in places where the soles of God's feet touch the ground. The stream flowing out from the grass on the mountain, as well as the taxi that appeared to fill our need for transportation expressed His presence with us in answer to our prayers.

CHAPTER THIRTY-THREE

Ruth's Poems

GOLDEN ANNIVERSARY REFLECTIONS

It's 50 grand years since my true love and I
took those vows that had meaning for life.

We only saw dimly what could lie
ahead for the two of us who became husband and wife.

It was warm love and then many surprises,
lots of hard work with its certain rewards.

Seven new babies came, then growing up years;
committees, volunteering and being on boards.

Vacations, ah yes, those family trips;
enjoying days off and always looking for more.

Sew it, mend it, fix it, shop for it too;
making sure time was never a bore.

Planting, milking, plowing and building---the future saw only
more of the same.

Hoeing and picking, freezing and canning;
every year more jobs entered life's game.

There was Sunday school and Bible school teaching;
get ready for this, get ready for that;

Will you please take me here, or may I go there?
Questions got harder each time they came back.

"Where did time go?" we say to each other.
I wish I could read all those stories again.

Each child needs attention. "Do you remember, did we warm
each child as does a good mother hen?"

There were eggs to gather, we did it together; corn to freeze--
-that pile looked horrendous;

Apple sauce, tomato juice, pod lima beans;
special times when Dad would come in to help us.

Up in the morning, checking the records at night;
ah, Dad was so faithful in working each day.

Discing and dreaming, will there be enough rain? Selling
chicks, buying tractors and making the hay.

Did he have any time for some fun on the side? November, December, oh, there was hunting.

The corn was all in. We said, "Go for it, Dad; we'll do the milking." Then, "When's he returning?"

It's rewarding, down deep in our hearts. As we look back, it wasn't all fun;

But what could prove in a greater way how God answered prayers in such a big sum?

Our family is precious, each one is so dear. The great grand-children keep coming, and each in their way

Warming our hearts, needing our prayers; with more reasons to trust in our Father each day.

April 1994
Ruth G. Rohrer

Eternity

Tell me—how many hours were there
Since God made earth and man?
Tell me, just tell me if you can.

So I ponder and I wonder
As my mind goes back and back;
But no one ever, ever
Can think back as far as that!
Tell me-------

How many happy hours will we be up in heaven?
Tell me, please tell me will it be more than seven?
Oh! Glory for God's children when all of us are gone;

The hours are never counted,
They'll go on and on and on!

Ruth G. Rohrer   1980

JUST THINKING

I like our lawn, the trees are tall,
The bushes shaped; I like it all.

The flowers have gone, the grass is mowed,
The borders trimmed, the bare twigs bowed.

It is December and I can wait.
What will come next? Snow on the gate?

The wind is blowing and I can sit;
The beauty and all---I just think about it.

Ruth Rohrer 1980

Grandpa is Special----A Tribute to Grandpa

"Elmer," that's who he was when he came to my door.

Upon asking, he answered, "My last name is Rohrer."

"Do you have plans for tonight?" his wishes implored.

"I'm scheduled at Vine Street to have Children's Meeting." And more!

"My sister, my cousin and Edith are waiting to go with me." I said.

"Could I be your chauffeur for such an occasion?" he pled.

"Well, yes, if this sounds good to you." And I fled to tell sister

And she told our cousin what the plans were instead.

"Oh no!" they decided. "If she has a date, let us just go to bed."

But I could not disappoint Edith, so the chauffeur did as he said.

Once a week this fine gentleman came to my door.

I liked him a lot more after each week, than before.

After two years the wedding bells finished that era of dating.

We became one and moved on a farm of high rating.

The name "Elmer" was followed in those years with "Daddy."

Two girls, then their brother and four more girls made him happy.

They played and they worked with him, one year to another;

With cows and chickens, in gardens and fields, along with their mother.

The years went so fast and soon it was time for another name change.

First it was Elmer, then Daddy---seven times in eleven years was the age range.

The new name came from a new generation. It was "Grandpa."

Did it fit? When he called me "Grandma" it gave verification.

After three precious toddlers came for a visit, I said to Grandpa,

"So glad we are young. Do you think this is it?"
Grandpa was wise. He knew we had girls.

Oh, sure there were more, and some even had curls.

The years passed---even thirty. Grandchildren were added.

They ran and they jumped until there were twenty.

Another name was coming. We still had to wait.

"Great Grandpa Rohrer." The honor truly was great!!

There are 14 of them now to call him that name.

His love stretches out as if it's a game.

But no, it's our heavenly Father who planned it that way.

I love him as Elmer, Daddy, Grandpa; and Great fits them all, I hasten to say!!

July 4, 2000   Ruth G. Rohrer

Celebrating my 90th birthday at the clubhouse at
Bahia Vista Estates, Sarasota, Florida.
They decorated my cake to look like a shuffleboard court.

L-R: Larry Neff, Michael Sauder, Norma Jean Neff, Clair Sauder, Elmer,
Ruth, Jay Rohrer, Nancy Sauder, Jane Rohrer

CHAPTER THIRTY-FOUR

In Conclusion

It was March 5, 2010 and the family was gathering at our Florida home. There seemed to be a festive spirit in the air. I now look back to my 90th birthday with fond memories as over 100 friends, along with some family members, gathered at the Bahia Vista Club House to celebrate my birthday. As we were driving home to Pennsylvania later that spring, our thoughts of down-sizing our living quarters seemed to come with a new intensity. The lawn and shrubbery were showing some neglect. But there was that wood shop—and I surely enjoyed it. We had put our name on the wait list at a couple of retirement communities and repeatedly said we were not ready to make the move. But this time it was different. It seemed so right and our children encouraged the move.

The willing hands of family and friends made it possible to

meet the deadline for a public sale. On October 28, 2010 we moved to Landis Homes Retirement Community, located on East Oregon Road, midway between our daughters, Nancy Sauder and Linda Landis. We soon found we were making new friends as well as getting better acquainted with former friends and even some relatives. The wood shop at Landis Homes also made me feel at home. It is in that shop that I continue to make Crokinole game boards and other small things. The staff and community members make this place a very desirable community with many activities from which to choose.

Ruth and I even now enjoy a good competitive game of shuffleboard or Crokinole. I can enjoy billiards or even the strategy involved in a game of Othello.

As we look back on these four short years living at Landis Homes, we conclude that, "Hitherto hath the Lord led us. Lead on, dear Father. Lead on."

Yes, Honey (my dear Ruth), we have been blessed. The road we have traveled has been joyful. As we round the bend in our journey, the evening sun lights up your face. It is beautiful to me! You have journaled our journey so well. You communicate love so well. I see it in our children and grands, and it's precious. You have poured out your life in such meaningful ways. I took so much for granted. Forgive me. I know you have. We are heaven bound and it is beautiful. We share the desire that Jesus shared in John 17: 20—23. "My prayer is not for them alone. I pray also for those who will believe in me through their message, that all of them may be one, Father, just as you are in me and I am in you. May they also be in us so that the world may believe that you have sent me. I have given them the glory that you gave me, that they may be one as we are one: I in them and you in me. May they be brought to complete unity to let the world know that you sent me and have loved them even as you have loved me."

I am very grateful to our Heavenly Father for leading me through this writing journey. May it be a help to others on their journey as well.

Here Ruth is reading an early draft of this book. I wrote my part in longhand on a tablet, and Ruth typed it. Nancy was our editor and "project manager."

Grandpa's Hunting Story

By Christina Landis Saxton

Written in Summer of 2008

Grandpa Rohrer chooses his words carefully. What I've always loved about my mom's side of the family is that his wife, his six daughters and his son make space for Grandpa's voice. Their reward, and mine, is his wit.

On holidays, three generations of his offspring gather around Grandma's dining room table. Grandpa always sits at the head with Grandma beside him. After we all settle in, and he has taken the traditional photo of the grand table setting, Grandpa usually asks one of the guests to pray for the meal. Sometimes we sing a hymn too.

As we pass the dishes around the table, banter, stories and laughter fill the air and good food fills our plates. But sometime between the first serving and dessert, one of the uncles will make mention of Grandpa's turkey story. Grandma will quickly echo, "Yes, we should hear the turkey story!" The words "turkey story" get passed around the table, and the kids quiet down. Everyone's attention focuses on Grandpa, who looks around with a smile in his eyes, as if to savor the presence of each person. He raises his hands slightly as he begins the story of this year's hunting adventure, which made a wild, mountain turkey into the meat we've been presently enjoying.

"As you may know, hunters must wear camouflage when hunting turkey. But you're also required to have a bright orange hat to alert the other hunters of where you are." Having given us some background knowledge, he starts the story. "I was hunting for turkey not far from the cabin. But instead of a turkey, a bear started coming my way. A black bear. Now, the only time a bear should be a problem, that is, a black bear, is if you would be situated between the mother and the baby."

(I silently marvel at the hunting trivia that I'm so glad my grandpa knows because it sounds like he was much more prepared to meet this bear than I would have been!)

Grandpa continues, "I didn't see a baby bear. And this bear, he just kept coming and coming towards me! At first, he didn't detect me, and I just let him come. But before long, he stood on his hind legs…and nuzzled my cap!"

"He actually nuzzled your cap, Daddy?" gasped Aunt Norma Jean, his oldest.

Calmly, Grandpa looked at my aunt, and then around the table, nodding his head with that smile still in his eyes. "Well, yes, he did," he replied.

"Well, what did you do?!?" exclaimed Aunt Esther.

Another nod and those lifted hands again. "Well," Grandpa said, "I went, 'WOOF'! And then the bear quietly got down and left."

"Woof!" repeated the grandkids, and the aunts start laughing at the thought of Grandpa saying 'Woof!' to a bear!

"Wait!" says an uncle, "how did this all happen?"

"Where was your hat?" others exclaimed, thinking that Grandpa might be keeping some of the story's details up his sleeve.

Grandpa nods his head and motions for us to quiet down. "Well, the hat was hanging on a tree about 15 feet away from me." And then, some more of that hunting knowledge, "The requirement is that the orange hat be within 15-20 feet of the hunter's location."

Grandpa's eyes don't just smile now, they twinkle. He is pleased that he managed to catch us with his story. And his chuckle joins that of the rest of us.

———

Down the Stairs to a Memory

Jewel Myers

Written February 25, 2011

Going to my grandparent's house was such an exciting and memorable time for me. We usually got there late at night after a long day of traveling. As we pulled up to their long driveway it was nearly impossible to hide my exhilaration. Once inside, I would quickly toss down all my bags, rush to the narrow door with a huge smile on my face and clunk down all the creaky wooden stairs to my grandparent's basement. The cool, slightly musty, air and rough concrete floor felt so familiar to me after all these years and, I called up the stairs hoping my brother would come down soon.

Looking around I would notice that not much had changed since the last time. Dingy windows and single light bulbs still lit up the room. Dusty canning jars and random tools still kept their places and no one had moved the old croquet set. I knew I could pick up right where I left off, although the paint was just a bit more faded on the shuffleboard court painted on the floor.

Last but definitely not least, after scanning the nostalgic room, my eyes would rest on the source of so much enjoyment: five old mattresses. Stained and having a distinct smell, these mattresses with broken springs and faded colors were my biggest and most remembered thing about my Grandparent's house.

People may say no one can learn anything from a basement, or even a place for that matter, but I strongly believe I gained so much from the time I spent there with my cousins. I learned how to work well with other people, use my imagination, and to respect other people's property.

Even though I lived in Tallahassee, Florida my whole life, my mom's family was from Lancaster, Pennsylvania. Roughly every year my family would pack up our many suitcases in the car and travel over 1,000 miles to Grandpa and Grandma's house. Built in 1973, my grandparent's house was not remarkably old, but it had stored up many fond memories over the years. For as long as I can remember, it was always overflowing with laughter.

Going down in my grandparent's basement was a magical novelty. Because of Florida's high water tables, I rarely saw basements. My grandparents used their basement as a storage room, like most people do. Having seven children, my grandparents had accumulated many boxes of things over the years. But one man's trash is another one's treasure and all of us grandchildren had the time of our lives exploring down there.

The biggest treasure for us grandchildren in the basement was the mattresses. Each time we went there we thought the mattresses must be moved around to a better position. We may have been small in size compared to the mattresses, but between determination and effort we finally got them moved around to just the right place. We always had some sort of disagreement about how they should be arranged; eventually we all learned to agree on a common place for each mattress.

Once the mattresses were in perfect order we worked on deciding what game to play. No matter how many disagreements and opinions we had, the game we chose would always become one of the favorite pastimes of the day. Because of these experiences down in the basement I am able to work together and get along with people much better than before. We put aside our differences and had lots of fun together.

Each time we went there our minds and imagination would go wild with ideas for new games to play. The games varied greatly, but they were mainly centered on using the mattresses, either for our homes, boats, doctor examination tables, or of course trampolines. Our most popular game was called "the animal game." Every one of the cousins would pick a favorite animal to be and choose a name. We lived together as families depending on what species each of us was, and each family had their own mattress. One mattress was yellow, so we called it the dessert. Another one was blue and it was the water. We had a mattress propped up against the wall and that was a tree for the birds. Then we would make up the game as we went along. Sometimes the carnivores would be nice, other times they would eat up all the peace-loving plant-eaters. The basement was one place my mind could thrive without limits; a place where I could have fun with my cousins and just be a kid.

Unfortunately when kids are kids it is not uncommon that something gets broken or someone gets hurt in the process of playing. It was no exception with us. I remember one or two times in the moment of having fun either I or one of my cousins had a careless moment and broke something. Our laughs would stop instantly and we would all stare at the broken object. We knew one of us would be trudging up those stairs to inform Grandma of the mishap. It was at times like this I learned that I should treat other people's things with as much care as if it were my own. Of course my grandma was extremely kind and helped us pick up the broken pieces. After that we were always much more careful with our game.

The basement at my grandparent's house was not just a playground for me, it was also a place to learn and grow, and I am very thankful for that. I gained skills for getting along with people; I learned how to use my imagination in a good way, and can now value other's things to take good care of them. I often find my mind drifting down those wooden stairs to a memory.

Hobbies and Highlights

Library shelves and table for Linda and Elmer's home.

Stools for the pool room at Landis Homes, built in the Landis Homes shop.

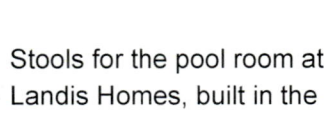

More Crokinole boards underway.

Flowers and yard work was always more fun than house-work!

Ruth still grows beautiful flowers at Landis Homes.

Our home on Charlestown Road, Lancaster, PA in the early 1950s.
We lived here from 1942—1973.

Aerial view of the farm in 1963.

Our home at 1270 Manor Blvd, Lancaster, PA
This was home from 1973-2011.

Our home in Bahia Vista
Estates, Sarasota, FL

We enjoyed spending
winters in Sarasota from
1996 until 2010.

Family Fun at William's Manor

Breakfast at the cabin— the table is crowded, the food always tastes good, and we usually run out of bacon.

The next generation gets a taste of "the cabin."

The tree stand is not really a deterrent. Still climbing at age 94. The great-grands climbed it, too.

Wrapping up a wonderful season of life.

Another successful hunt at William's Manor.

Shuffleboard is popular at William's Manor.

Fun with the Grands

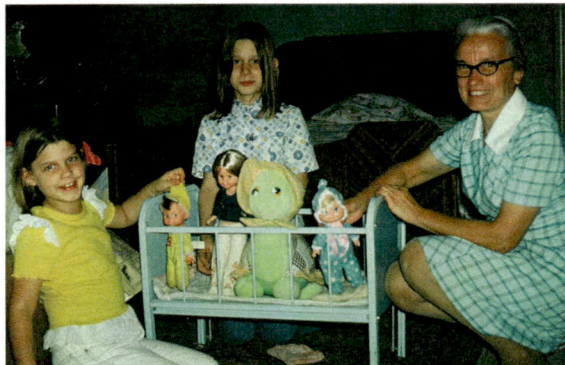

Amy and Becky Rohrer play with dolls, using the little bed their aunts used before them.

Julie Neff shows Grandma how to keep jumping—maybe how to stay young, too.

Becky, Matt and Amy Rohrer have a tea party at Grandma Garber's house.

Our first grandchild, Becky Rohrer Rogers, came to celebrate our 65th anniversary.

We usually played games into the night when the family went to William's Manor.

What goes around comes around— I combed Grandma Garber's hair, and here Debbie and Rachel Landis combed my hair.

Joe Landis keeps me sharp playing Othello. We each win some.

A pile of cousins at our Florida home. L-R: Debbie Landis, Rachel Landis, Jewel Myers, Andrew Foronda, Joe Landis, Alyssa Foronda. These are six of our youngest grandchildren.

Here is part of the crew who went to the cabin in 2014. The cabin sleeps 20 or so comfortably, but we usually push the limits, and fill the floor and sofas, too.

I built this gun cabinet for Jay after I had a mini stroke. The challenge was good therapy for me.

I made this copy of the umbrella stand that held Ruth's daddy's hat when he courted Ruth's mother. Our daughter Vera has the original piece now, and this copy is in Norma Jean's home.

Sale day—the family all pitched in to help.

Several of the grands helped as runners for the sale. Here Andrew Foronda and Joe Landis check things out.

None of us ever put a book together before, but we had a good time working as a team.

We welcomed great-grand number 27 in April 2015. Here we get our first look at Tamara Ruth Saxton when she was three weeks old.

Staying in touch from the hospital room, May 2015.

Debbie Landis, Rachel Nowakowski and Nancy

checking progress on this book.

A note from the Editor

While working with my parents on this project I was challenged, enlightened, sometimes frustrated, and sometimes surprised. Mother has always been a writer – the travel journals included in this book are evidence of that. But Daddy – well, we rarely saw more than a signature from Daddy over the years. When he started writing his memories on a tablet in the summer of 2014 we were all astonished! He said he thought he shouldn't wait any longer to get started.

Little did we know how quickly things would change. On March 5, 2015, we celebrated Daddy's 95th birthday. The season's biggest snowstorm didn't keep him from going out for breakfast. Now, in mid May of the same year, he is quickly fading, and looking forward to meeting his Maker in Glory.

Mother is strong, spending as much time with Daddy as possible, in spite of having had surgery herself just a few weeks ago. Ever the supportive and encouraging helpmeet, Mother still gets a sparkle in her eye that matches the smile on Daddy's face when they see one another. Their enduring love is a treasure to observe.

What a privilege it has been for me to learn to know my parents more intimately through working on their life stories with them. I heard some of their stories for the first time; many of them are included here. I came to understand Daddy's strong sense of right and wrong and Mother's dedication to serving others in new ways.

Mother and Daddy give all the credit to God for their rich and joyful (but not always happy, they emphasize) life. They want the reader to know their lives were not flawless, their judgment not always sound, their choices not always the very best. But they both strove to bring honor to God, and feel blessed now, in their golden years. May you, the reader, also be blessed by their stories.

— Nancy Rohrer Sauder

Acknowledgments

We are the authors of this story. The word pictures we painted carry you from our earliest memories to our experiences in 2015. We have many people to thank for bringing us to this point in time. God gave us loving parents and the Holy Spirit has led us step by step. Sometimes we obeyed and other times we chose our own paths.

We give deep appreciation to our daughter Nancy, who helped us refine and edit our manuscripts. She was our encourager along the way, telling us, "Yes, people want to read your story." Many friends have encouraged us along the way. We also appreciate the help that came from our daughter Linda and her husband Elmer Landis, who helped with proofreading.

Thank you to God for His unspeakable gift for us all.

Elmer and Ruth

Note: Elmer H Rohrer died on May 16, 2015. His long and generous life reflected his love for God and his family. He treasured relationships above things. He will be missed, and his mark will be carried on by those who loved him.

In spite of a marathon proofreading session outside his room at Landis Homes, this book was not ready for print before he died. But Elmer approved the back cover only a day before he went to Glory.